P9-APR-346

WITHDRAWN

# Black and White Together

## *The Search for Common Ground*

Danny Duncan Collum

ORBIS BOOKS
**Maryknoll, New York 10545**

The Catholic Foreign Mission Society of America (Maryknoll) recruits and trains people for overseas missionary service. Through Orbis Books, Maryknoll aims to foster the international dialogue that is essential to mission. The books published, however, reflect the opinions of their authors and are not meant to represent the official position of the society.

Copyright © 1996 by Danny Duncan Collum

Published by Orbis Books, Maryknoll, NY 10545-0308

All rights reserved. No part of this publication may be reproduced or transmitted in any form or by any means, electronic or mechanical, including photocopying, recording, or any information storage or retrieval system, without prior permission in writing from the publishers.

Queries regarding rights and permissions should be addressed to: Orbis Books, P.O. Box 308, Maryknoll, NY 10545-0308.

Manufactured in the United States of America

**Library of Congress Cataloging-in-Publication Data**

Collum, Danny Duncan.
    Black and white together : the search for common ground / Danny Duncan Collum.
       p.   cm.
    Includes index.
    ISBN 1-57075-097-1 (alk. paper)
    1. United States—Race relations.   2. Poor—United States—History.   3. Afro-Americans—Economic conditions.  I. Title.
E185.615.C644   1996
305.8′00973—dc20                96-18833
                                  CIP

*To my parents, Murray and Martha Collum,*
*and my teacher, Billy Ray Hicks*

# Contents

# Preface

I was born into a white working-class family in the Mississippi Delta. My grandparents on both sides had been sharecroppers. The year of my birth was 1954, just a couple of months before the U.S. Supreme Court announced the Brown vs. Board of Education decision that outlawed school segregation. The year after I was born, Emmett Till was killed in the next county over from ours.

My hometown is called Greenwood. In 1962, when I was eight, a white man from Greenwood named Byron De La Beckwith drove down to Jackson and killed Medgar Evers, a black man who was the head of the Mississippi NAACP. Everyone in Greenwood knew that he did it, but at the time Beckwith got off with a hung jury. He didn't go to jail until thirty years later, when everything had changed.

In 1964 my hometown was also one of the centers of action for Freedom Summer. In 1970, when I was in the tenth grade, the schools of my hometown were finally integrated. At the start of the Christmas break there were two high schools in town, one black and one white. In January there was one school, half black and half white. It was a different world for everyone, except for the more affluent people who sent their children to the new all-white, private school on the outskirts of town.

Where I come from my people were taught to look down upon black folks as lesser beings. When I was a child they taught that to me. But from that same upbringing I also learned that there were people out there—other white people

—who also looked down on us. In the middle of all that they taught me to sing, "Red and yellow, black and white, they are precious in his sight, Jesus loves the little children of the world." And they taught me to pledge solemn allegiance to a flag that represented "liberty and justice for all."

I have spent much of my life trying to make some meaning from this great confusion about race and class and religion and democracy. This book is one result of that effort. It is not a systematic analysis of race and class in America. I am not qualified for that. I am not a sociologist, or an economist, or even a historian. I am a writer, a Catholic Christian, and a citizen, and I do what I can do.

What I do here is mainly tell some stories which, I think, suggest some of the better possibilities that reside among us. At a time when so many of our worst possibilities are so readily on display, that seems worth the doing. In his landmark book, *Race Matters,* Cornel West wrote, "In these downbeat times, we need as much hope and courage as we do vision and analysis." He also suggested that "the most valuable sources for help, hope and power consist of ourselves and our common history." I have taken that quotation as my charge.

This book contains some of the stories and characters and ideas that I have encountered in my own two decades of wrestling with these questions. The scope of the book is limited by my experience. It is no more comprehensive than it is systematic. For instance, much of it is rooted in the South, and it deals with race as a matter involving African Americans and white people.

Of course, until the urban uprisings of the late 1960s, when you talked about a "race question" most people assumed that you meant blacks and whites in the South. Things are more complicated now. But I believe that our patterns of thought and models of action are still rooted in that original confrontation of black and white, which in turn has its roots in the South and in slavery. That is still what we Americans talk about when we talk about race.

# Acknowledgments

Eighteen long years ago *Sojourners* magazine was looking for someone who could think about art and politics and type at the same time. That's when Ed Spivey, the magazine's art director, asked me to try my hand at a film review. The result was my first published writing. Thanks, Ed. It's always nice to be asked.

That first review was about *Blue Collar,* a Paul Schrader film in which black and white auto-workers struggled with their common enemies and their own deep divisions. This book has been in the works for at least that long. To go back even further, this book reflects twenty-five years of political discussions with my friend Perry Perkins who is now an Industrial Areas Foundation organizer in New Orleans.

In addition, professors Michael Cowan and Barbara Ewell at Loyola University in New Orleans steered me toward some of the material for the early chapters. Anthony Parker, then an editor at *Sojourners,* solicited my essay on racism (in the August, 1990 issue) from which this book ultimately grew.

In this book I strive to be optimistic, or at least hopeful, about our common human, and American, possibilities. That hope ultimately rests on faith, and for me it has been undergirded by my membership in Our Lady of Lourdes Church in New Orleans and Our Lady Queen of Peace in Arlington, Virginia, and by my occasional visits to St. Ann's of Carthage, Mississippi. My thanks to the people, priests, and religious of those interracial parish communities.

My wife, Polly Duncan Collum, read everything in this book, repeatedly. The first draft bears her pencil slashes across almost every page. She challenged weak arguments, tried to keep me to a consistent tone, and corrected most of my errors in punctuation and grammar. Polly is professionally employed in Catholic social ministry and her work inevitably fed into this one. Our shared commitment to a Catholic vision of community is at the heart of this book, and at the center of the home we share with our children, Christopher and Magdalena.

# CHAPTER 1

# A Time of Reckoning

## Scenes from the Nineties

It was a cool, clear Monday morning in October 1995. At 9:00 A.M. traffic was unusually light on the Shirley Highway, a short stretch of interstate that runs from I-95 to the Washington Mall. I was driving north, sailing along at 65 m.p.h. I'd dropped my son at pre-school and was thinking about my morning's work. Along the way I passed a white four-door Japanese sedan with Florida tags. Inside the car were four young black men.

"Cocaine highway," I muttered to myself. It was an ugly thought, sparked by the ugly fact that young black men in late-model sedans were often employed to transport drugs up the I-95 corridor from south Florida to the teeming markets of the urban East. The guys in the Hyundai fit the profile used by state police all along the seaboard. Still, facts or no facts, it was an ugly thought and I knew it.

Then, in the very same instant, I remembered another fact. This was the day of the Million Man March. That's why the traffic was so light. Commuters were taking the trains, or staying home, to avoid the massive tie-up around the Mall. That was also the most likely reason why those four guys from Florida were cruising north at this hour.

On second glance, those young men might well have been college students. They had probably driven all night for the

1

chance to join other black men in "a day of atonement and reconciliation." Along the way they might have been stopped and searched by state policemen looking for young black drug carriers.

Like a lot of people, I was skeptical about the value of the Million Man March, and downright cynical about the leadership offered by Nation of Islam minister Louis Farrakhan. I still am. But in that moment on Shirley Highway I had to admit that the marchers had a point. There I was confronted with the fact that, at some level, I too perceived black men, especially young ones, as deviants and thugs. I was also confronted with the fact that some of those young black men were taking positive action to change that perception. There was something immensely moving about this, Farrakhan be damned.

That night I tried to tell this story to my white and mostly affluent college writing students. Their cynicism was invincible. "That's just sentiment," one of them said, hurling the ultimate expletive of our day. "Tomorrow you could see those same guys and think the same thing you first thought and you'd probably be right," another added. "They probably *were* on a drug run and just stopped off at the march."

"But nobody's life is that simple," I tried to respond. "Even guys who are mixed up with drugs, aren't *just* drug dealers."

The students' perceptions of the Million Man March were entirely about Farrakhan's sexism, homophobia, racism and anti-Semitism—all the same things I worried about. "But even Farrakhan has another side," I tried to remind them. "He's also a musician—a calypso singer and a violinist—and a good one."

A few days earlier I had been in the supermarket at 1:00 P.M. Eastern time. While I was searching through the cereal aisle, a voice came over the store loudspeaker. The announcement wasn't about a car parked in the fire lane, or a special on day-old bread. "Ladies and gentlemen," the voice said loudly, "we have a verdict in the O.J. Simpson trial. O.J. is not guilty!"

Most of the people in the store at the time, customers and staff alike, were black and they cheered, openly and loudly, the way people do at ball games. The white people, myself included, looked at the floor and made our purchases in awkward silence.

All over the country different versions of that scene played themselves out. That evening the pictures bounced off satellites and hummed across the fiber-optic cables of our global grapevine. All the reports said the same thing. For almost a year the popular culture of the nation had been saturated with a single crime story. Millions of Americans had watched the same murder trial every day on the same handful of media outlets. Yet black and white Americans seemed to have witnessed different trials, perhaps on different planets. Responses to the verdict were diametrically opposed and the rift ran right along the color line.

Race is back at the center of American public life. On that almost everyone can agree. From the dramatic—and media—events cited above to racially charged debates about welfare, crime, and affirmative action, there is no avoiding the question of color. In fact, historians may someday see 1995 as a year when America entered another tortuous day of reckoning with the terrible legacy of African enslavement.

The ingredients for a new time of reckoning have been brewing at least since the great reversal of the early 1980s, when the federal government began to withdraw from its commitments to civil rights and the social safety net. The tension multiplied in the later 1980s when crack cocaine moved into the economic void of inner-city America and brought with it an explosion of criminal violence.

In the wake of these social disasters the African American community became, in the white popular mind, firmly identified with welfare, drugs, and crime. Never mind that most welfare recipients were still white, or that young black people actually used drugs—all drugs, including cigarettes and alcohol—at much lower rates than their white counterparts.

The 1992 Rodney King uprising in Los Angeles was an angry harbinger of things to come. But that warning bell went unheeded and by mid-decade tempers seemed shorter, walls between the races seemed higher, and the dream of a common American destiny was fading fast.

We have faced these periods of reckoning before in U.S. history, most dramatically in the post-Civil War Reconstruction era of 1865–1876 and again in the civil rights years of 1954–1968. Both of those periods were marked at the outset by rising aspirations for a truly multiracial American democracy. Both ended in tragedy and defeat.

**Classes and Colors**

The good news about today's racial turmoil is that the silence has been broken. We are talking about race as a fact of American life. We are trying, again, to come to terms with our past and see what it means for our future. We are assessing the progress, or lack thereof, since the civil rights years. This discussion is taking place in settings high and low, from the daytime talk shows to the halls of academe.

The bad news is that most of our talk about race makes little sense. Too much of it is an emotional exchange of blame and invective. The rest is often an abstract discussion about values and perceptions that only rarely touches base with economic or cultural realities.

On the Right it is assumed that black America's persistent poverty and unemployment are caused by failures of character which can be cured only by harsh discipline and stern sermonizing. This stance seems grounded in a view of the African American community as the carrier of a social pathology of drugs, crime, and sexual license that infects the broader culture.

This view provides a neat rationale for cutting social welfare spending and locking up minor drug offenders. But it has little relationship to the economic realities faced by uneducated and unskilled young people. And, worse still, it falsifies the story of American culture since the 1960s.

For instance, the drug trade, which lies at the heart of violent urban crime, is not the creation of black America. Its roots are in the mainstream of American middle-class culture.

In the past decade young black men, denied other economic prospects, have taken up positions as street-level merchandisers and enforcers for the drug trade. But this underground industry is founded on the fast-living tastes of an affluent and endlessly pleasure-seeking America that is predominantly white. The roots of the drug trade are not in the inner city but in the so-called counterculture of white baby boomers' indulgent youth.

Likewise family breakdown, which has occupied center stage in recent welfare debates, is not a racial phenomenon. Over the years there have been differences between black and white American family patterns owing to the forced family break-ups caused by slavery. But the much-discussed breakdown of the black family in the past three decades is a different matter. This has been simply one highly visible, and widely scapegoated, symptom of a color blind cultural epidemic.

This epidemic, too, started at the top of American society in the 1960s, with the "sexual revolution" and divorce law reforms. Out-of-wedlock births have risen sharply across the board, among all racial and economic groupings. The consequences of loosened family bonds have been more severe at the bottom of society, where people can ill afford this brand of individualism. But even here the relevant factor is poverty, not race. In those predominantly white communities where poverty is as dire and intense as it is in the non-white inner cities, the rates of illegitimacy and teen motherhood are comparable.

The "values talk" of America's cultural conservatives is designed to demonstrate that race is no longer a significant factor in the disproportionate poverty and pain suffered by black America. In fact, this talk only projects the cultural failings of the majority onto a relatively powerless and vulnerable minority. In the process it inadvertently demonstrates how alive and well racism still is among us. "Values talk" also evades the economic realities of an economy in which low-skill, entry-level jobs have disappeared at a dismaying rate and real wages for all but the most affluent are in decline.

Even the two great racial touchstone events of 1995 with which we began tell of realities that run deeper than race. The Million Man March was framed in terms of cultural values. Many of these values are the same as those touted by the Republican Revolution—self-reliance, restraint, responsibility. After all, Farrakhan is nothing if not a cultural conservative. This was the greatest appeal of the march. It said to the world that, although black Americans did not make their own social problems, they could take the lead in solving them.

Of course, the other cultural reference point for the Million Man March was race-based nationalism. For Farrakhan and many of his nationalist followers there is a sense of cultural superiority attached to the biological fact of African ancestry. This brand of Afrocentrism understandably plays well with people who have for centuries been systematically stripped of their cultural legacy and their self-esteem. Within limits, nationalism can offer some resources for countering the symptoms of African America's cultural crisis. But the racial limitations of nationalism prevent it from seriously addressing the economic crisis that faces black men, women, and children at the turn of this century.

This economic crisis is the same one that faces all Americans, of all colors, who lack advanced degrees and professional skills. The jobs that many of these people traditionally performed may have been hard and dirty but, especially in heavily unionized basic industries, those jobs paid a family wage and provided a foothold on the American economic ladder. Those jobs have been disappearing for more than twenty years and today they are all but gone.

This national crisis is a catastrophe for black people. For most of their history in this country African Americans were not allowed onto the ladder at all. Then, just as they began to gain full access, the bottom rungs were pulled off. In these circumstances, Farrakhan's racial rhetoric provides a catharsis for black anger while diverting his constituency away from the underlying sources of its problems. This is, of course, the same purpose served in the white political mainstream by racially coded rhetoric about welfare and crime. The rhetoric diverts working-class white Americans away from the economic facts of their lives.

Most media discussion of the O.J. Simpson case took place in the slippery realm of racial perceptions. The great controversy was about the very different ways that whites and blacks "perceived" the facts of the case and the outcome of the trial. Viewed through this lens the case did dramatize deep racial divisions. But one could just as easily have viewed the case as a dramatic demonstration of American racial progress. A black man was charged with killing a blonde, white woman. There was, at least, strong evidence against him but the presumption of innocence held. That would probably not have happened thirty years ago.

The presumption of innocence held for Simpson because the police and the prosecution made serious errors of procedure and strategy, and mostly because Simpson could afford the legal talent and person-hours to capitalize on those mistakes. The only thing Simpson's trial really proved was that, at least when it comes to litigation, money is more important than skin color. This lesson about economic power was all but obscured in the rush to racialize the case.

The point here is that today much of our public discussion about race is really misdirected talk about economic class. It is talk about how to mitigate, or contain, or exploit, the worst effects of economic decline and cultural drift on those Americans who, because they are the poorest, are also most vulnerable.

**Division and Domination**

The discussions and controversies of the recent past may have almost convinced many of us that race and racial divisions are the most important facts about American life. This is, of course, more than half true. Racial oppression and discrimination have been persistent themes throughout 400 years of American history. Any attempt to sort out the roots of our present problems must take that into account. For instance, as already noted, past and present racism is certainly at work in the cultural scapegoating of black America and in the apportionment of economic pain.

But many of the forces at work in American life today have little to do with race except insofar as racial obsessions and racial rhetoric can become obstacles to facing reality. Sorting those out will be difficult. Yet if we look and listen, with open minds and honest hearts, we will see that race is central to American history and culture, and to some of our current social problems. Nevertheless the questions of race, in our past and present, are not inescapable and all-consuming. We are not bound and circumscribed by them.

Today we are tempted to think of America's racial divisions as permanent things. We seem to think that, like the poor, they have always been with us and always will be. And that may lead us to think that there is little that can be done about them. But America's racial conflicts, and even our racial categories, were not simply decreed by fate or handed down on stone tablets. Our racial definitions, attitudes, and patterns evolved out of a specific set of historical circumstances. They evolved to serve the ongoing Anglo-American purpose of economic exploitation, first of a continent, then of a world.

From the time that the first Africans were brought to these shores, race has served as a wedge to keep American workers divided for the benefit of owners. Race serves to limit our capacity for collective action and to thwart the full economic expression of America's potentially dangerous democratic ideals. So it was in the days of slavery, during the birth of industrialism in the nineteenth century, and in the fundamental economic struggles of the 1930s. So it is today in a time of American economic decline and disinvestment.

Race is a tool. It is a very sophisticated tool. It works in the mind and the spirit, and it sounds the primal cries of blood and sex. But it is still a tool, an invented device, used to serve a larger end.

Over the centuries of American history, race has taken on a life of its own. False and demeaning racist mythologies about black people are deep and virulent in the minds of all white Americans. White folk all, to one degree or another, are indoctrinated with lies about black people's character, their intellectual and emotional lives, and their sexuality. This mythology has been planted in our heads to make us think that we are some sort of masters and "they" deserve to be slaves.

American white racist mythology has its own autonomous power and its own secret life among us. White racist mythology is best described using the religious language of the demonic. And it must be attacked and broken through warfare that is cultural, psychological, and spiritual. But, given all that, racism still cannot be attacked successfully outside of the context of its creation. And that context is one of color-coded myth-making done in the hard-headed service of economic exploitation.

Race is, and always has been, a tool of economic domination. It is used to ensure the existence of a very cheap, and—one way or another—captive, black work force at the bottom of the social ladder. It is also used today, as it always has been, to give white workers a sense of relative advantage that keeps them happy with something less than full equity and true democracy.

In the economic good times, the race myth provides the working majority with the identity of "white" as a consolation prize when they are denied access to a full share of wealth and power. In the bad times it can provide them with a scapegoat, someone to blame, other than the boss or the system.

Today the good times are over. Since 1973 the American economy has been characterized by a big freeze on wages and a big squeeze on living standards. In the Reaganaut eighties this change was accompanied by a shift of public resources to the rich (in tax breaks) and a corresponding cut in practical programs to support the poor (for instance, public housing) and the middle class (college financial aid) or both (all aid to public education).

The central—and these days mostly ignored—task in overcoming racism is to get ordinary people to think about themselves not exclusively in terms of their relationship to other ethnic groups, but in terms of their relationship to the economic and social forces that rule their lives.

Today this means asking questions such as, "Who decided we live in a global economy?" "Where's the trickle that was supposed to come down from business incentives?" "Why do the good jobs have to go overseas and the lousy ones stay here?" "Who's flipping the switches in the information age?"

These questions are immensely more relevant to the crack-ridden and disinvested plight of the inner city than any amount of nationalist self-affirmation. They also speak directly to the strained families and faded hopes of white ethnic neighborhoods, to the two (or more) jobs-per-household suburbs, and to the formerly farm-centered and dying rural communities.

The old saying is that when white America sneezes, black America catches cold. But the economic storm of the past twenty years has given even the white middle class a lingering and debilitating cold that won't go away, and it has left African America with a crippling case of pneumonia.

One patient is in worse shape than the other, but both diseases result from the same set of environmental causes. However, instead of joining up to remedy our common condition, we keep comparing symptoms, and getting sicker.

## A Moral Umbrella

Of course there has to be a moral context for taking on the issue of racism in America, some overarching canopy of values under which all people of good will can gather. That was the special genius of the civil rights movement from 1955 to 1965. From the social morality of the Bible and the American democratic tradition, that movement fashioned a new American civil religion that provided the moral foundation for far-reaching so-

cial change. The rhetoric and practice of the civil rights movement gave the majority of Americans a sense of a shared attach-
ment to a common good. During the best days of the
movement, ordinary people felt that they were being addressed
on the basis of their common humanity and called to partici-
pate in a common destiny, one shared by all Americans.

It was a big and durable moral umbrella that the civil
rights movement created. Today, thirty years later, it is commonly noted by political thinkers, from the president on
down, that we Americans are afflicted by a lack of community
ties and a withered perception of the common good. We lack a
defining sense of belonging to something larger than ourselves. In this regard, the political style and language created
during the civil rights years is still quite relevant. That umbrella still works, and we can still use it, if we ever become interested in unity and community again.

But a compelling moral framework alone is not enough to
tackle the question of race in America. The history of the civil
rights movement also suggests that in order to become politically functional, our sense of the common good must be
grounded in concrete social and economic reality. Our common vision and commonly held values must be grounded in
the bedrock of common interests if we are to dismantle a struc-
ture of racist attitudes and practices that is founded on economic division and rivalry.

This was where the civil rights movement stalled. There
was agreement between Southern blacks and affluent Northern liberals that Cold War America had to be purged of segregation and black disenfranchisement. Everyone agreed that
the blatant bad behavior of the Southern white establishment
had to end. But once those goals were accomplished consensus in the movement evaporated, and so did Northern liberal
support.

In those days, in the late 1960s, the movement faced the
choice of becoming a class-based alliance for democratic re-
newal, or a race-based movement building enclaves of black
power. It split both ways at once and succeeded at neither. This

was in no small part because the power of the federal government, which partly allied itself with the early phases of the civil rights campaign, brought down its full repressive weight upon both tendencies.

Today we live pressed against the limits hit by the civil rights movement. Reflexive reference to the glory days of 1955–1965 can be inspiring or consoling. But those years hold little practical help for us now. We must instead pick up where things were left off, around April 4, 1968, and look for a new way forward. And we must do so without the comforting cushion of 1960s-era economic expansion.

In this context, guilt-tripping and race-baiting—of all stripes—can only deepen divisions and cast people more firmly into their respective racial mindsets. If racism was created on the ground of a specific set of historical, economic interests, then it must be successfully attacked on that same ground. Racism must be attacked by replacing false divisions and false rivalries of race or color with the real, tangible common ground of shared values and interests. This includes the clear economic self-interest that is shared by the vast majority of Americans, of all colors and ethnicities, who are not rich, and whose standard of living is now in decline.

### The Power of a Common Story

In recent decades much time and energy has been spent in debunking the standard version of U.S. history and writing back into the story the oppression and persecution experienced by racial minorities and indigenous people. This has been an important and necessary process, and one that must continue. But the process of debunking has also helped to obscure the moments in our history when Americans have done better and the promise of a multiracial cooperative commonwealth has, however briefly, taken on flesh among us. We need today to be reminded that our history is not simply the story of oppression and victimization. It also contains a strong counter-heritage of solidarity and resistance. This American story, even when it is ambiguous and conflicted, is our greatest strength and the repository of our most powerful common values.

Included in this counter-heritage are stories, dating from the dawn of American time to the present, that push us past the limits of race and suggest a way forward. It is time to tell those stories again. If there is a way forward, it will be found by following the best unrealized hopes and dreams of our past, and by building upon the few small victories for human community that do lie there, obscured by time and ideological neglect.

These are stories of ordinary white and black Americans coming together and forming alliances to struggle for a more just distribution of wealth and power. The black people in these stories all knew the experience of slavery, and so knew enough to be suspicious of any white man's claims. But they ultimately did not let suspicion limit their field of action or their vision of the possible. They suspected, and rightly so, that freedom is indivisible, and must be won for all, together.

The white people in these stories were not the enlightened, dissident children of the professional classes. They were not the New England abolitionists, or the white Northern college students of 1964. These were ordinary, relatively unschooled, poor or working-class white people. Often they were people who had been raised with generations of racist mythology, even cloaked in the guise of the Christian religion. But, at certain points in space and time, those ordinary white, working-class Americans ignored the overbearing voices of division and hatred and managed to hear the heartbeat of common humanity.

**A Family Reunion**

In March, 1988 I went home to Mississippi to write about Jesse Jackson and his Rainbow Coalition campaign for the Democratic presidential nomination. As part of that campaign, Jackson addressed a rally at Mississippi State University in Starkville, Mississippi. Mississippi State is not the first place most people would look for a new social vision. It is what is unkindly called a "cow college." Its distinctly non-elite student body is mostly drawn from the farms and small towns of the Magnolia State.

On that day, even before Jackson was scheduled to arrive, the campus auditorium was filled far beyond capacity with a crowd that was roughly equal parts black and white. One young white woman attended the rally with her black friend. The white woman was as country as country could be. But she liked Jesse Jackson, she said, because her daddy was a farmer and Jackson was the only one that year talking about what was happening to the farmers.

When the rally finally got under way, a local Starkville elected official, a black man in his thirties, took the podium and began his remarks by quoting from rhythm and blues singer/songwriter Sam Cooke's posthumous classic "A Change Is Gonna Come." That song fused sacred and secular musical traditions into an anthem-like evocation of the struggle to be human and free. It began with the simple line, "I was born by the river, in a little tent, and just like that river, I've been running ever since...."

In the spirit of Sam Cooke's pop song, Jackson's remarks that day took the political stump speech places it was never meant to go. Along the way he touched chords that resonated with the fundamental mystery and promise of American life. Much of Jackson's podium time that day was taken up by his standard campaign address, one that he was giving several times a day, seven days a week. But about halfway into his Starkville speech, Jackson departed from his standard text and delivered a new, perhaps even improvised, piece of political poetry.

When the cheering had died down after one of his standard applause lines, Jackson stood straight at the rostrum and drew a deep breath. He looked out over the small sea of black and white Southerners gathered before him and said:

We're gathered here today in search of something. ...We're like lost brothers and sisters who were orphaned off at childbirth because something happened to our parents. And we never really knew who we were....

But then someplace along the way we bumped into each other. What a strange sensation! We resembled each other. Our interests are the same. The rhythm of our talking is much the same. The more we talk the more our curiosity is aroused. We begin to find that both have been adopted. Then we start searching for our parents, and we find them. Then we search for our brothers and our sisters. And we find that we're each other's brother. We're each other's sister.

And now here we are in this family reunion. This is the New South. This is the New Mississippi. This is the heartbeat of the New America.

In that moment Jackson summed up the horror and the hope of race relations in America. We are, in the cold, new world of the 1990s, orphaned children of the same sad and beautiful history. To know how we can proceed together, we will need to know how it was that we, who have so much in common, were so torn apart. Many of the answers to that mystery lie buried almost 400 years beneath our feet, in the early days of the Virginia colony and the first sustained encounter of black and white in our part of the New World.

As historian Wesley Frank Craven has written, to talk about seventeenth-century Virginia is to talk about the South before it was, consciously, the South. It is also to talk about race in a time before racial categories, codes, and customs were so rigidly defined. Looking back at those days, we can't help but remember all that was to come. The events in the Virginia colony set us down the road to slavery, war, segregation and brutality. But we may still learn something new if we look back at those times for signs of what might have been, and what still could be.

CHAPTER 2

# Revolt before Race

*The Unity of Servitude in Old Virginia*

### William and Mary Were Lovers...

It was a Sunday morning in the Anglican parish church of Elizabeth River, Virginia. The service began with the singing of a hymn. The congregation, numbering a couple of dozen, stood in the pews, prayer books in hand. Most of the people were dressed poorly in rough and ragged woolen clothes. Near the front of the church there were two families wearing silks and satins from the old country. Almost all of the parishioners, rich and poor alike, were English folk come to take their chances in a strange New World.

The more comfortable families at the front were big landowners. They grew tobacco, as nearly everyone did in seventeenth-century Virginia. In those days Virginia money consisted of notes promising the delivery of a certain number of pounds of tobacco. Most of the other worshipers at Elizabeth River were white indentured servants. They had been brought from England in chains to do the intensive, back-breaking work of tobacco cultivation. They served for a term of several years. At the end of the term they were free to try and find their way in the New World alone.

A few of the Elizabeth River parishioners were freedmen, former servants now struggling to get a foothold. By 1649 land in the settled coastal areas of Virginia was already becoming scarce, at least compared to the open bounty of the first decades. There was plenty of land further inland, but there were also plenty of Indians to defend it.

Scattered among these various classes of English were several Africans. Africans were still few in number in Virginia. They had first arrived thirty years before, when twenty of them had been purchased off a Dutch merchant ship that was passing from the Caribbean to New Amsterdam. Some of the Africans in Virginia were slaves for life, as they had been in the Caribbean. Some of them worked under the usual terms of indenture. Others had earned their freedom and even owned small parcels of land. Elsewhere in the colony there were even free Africans who themselves owned servants.

On this particular morning, the Elizabeth River minister faced his motley congregation and said the familiar prayers. The people mumbled their responses, but none of them were really looking at their prayer books. All eyes were fixed on the center aisle of the church. There, atop two small stools, a young man and woman were standing. Each was wrapped from head to toe in a white cotton sheet. Each held a long white rod, or wand, in their right hand. This was the customary punishment for a couple caught in fornication. Later in the service the couple would be directed to recite words of penance before the assembly. If the couple persisted in their activity and were found out again, they might be publicly whipped. Everyone in the parish knew this. It was routine—as routine as the ceaseless rushing of human desire.

The couple standing in the aisle on this particular day were named William and Mary. William Watts was a small farmer of the region, formerly a servant, now a free white man. The woman was Mary, still a servant, and an African. It was 1649. Two centuries later, in at least half the states of the new American republic, miscegenation would be either an evil secret or a deadly crime. But in 1649 the black woman and the white man were not master and slave. They were not racial criminals. They were just a couple of lovers caught in the act.

Change the scene now, to Linhaven village in Norfolk County, Virginia, a few decades later, in 1681. The New World was a little bit older. The black population was larger and race consciousness was more evident in the society and its institutions. Already blacks had lost some of their legal rights. For instance, slaves were no longer automatically freed when they converted to Christianity, and free blacks were not allowed to own white servants. In 1669 a law was passed stating that a slave owner who killed a defiant slave was not guilty of a felony.

But some things did not change. In the court of Lower Norfolk in 1681 we could find another couple, again named William and Mary. Mary Williamson, a single white woman, was in love with William, "a negro," and their expressions of love had come to light.

For the crime of fornication, Mary Williamson was charged a fine amounting to 500 pounds of tobacco. William, her lover, had no resources to pay a fine. He also had plainly irritated the authorities. He must have earlier refused his penance in church. In passing sentence, the county judge said that William had "very arrogantly behaved himself in Linhaven Church in the face of the congregation." As a result he received the harsher penalty of thirty lashes upon his bare back.

Certainly thirty lashes was a severe punishment for the charges levied against William. We can guess that prejudice related to his color entered into the judgment. But 150 years later, or 250 years later, for that matter, William would certainly have been killed for this offense, and killed in the most brutal fashion.

**Toward Freedom ... Together**

Look back even further now, to 1640. Before the General Court of Virginia, Captain William Pierce complained that "six of his servants and a negro of Mr. Reynold's had plotted to run away unto the Dutch plantation." The court found that six white servants and Emanuel, "the foresaid negro ... did take the skiff of the said Captain Pierce, their master, and

corn, powder and shot and guns...." The men then sailed together all the way "down to the Elizabeth River." There they
were captured.

The court ordered that all seven men be punished with
"30 stripes and the letter R [for runaway] burned into the
cheek." The ringleader of the uprising, Christopher Miller, a
white man, and Emanuel, the African, were also sentenced to
work for one year in chains.

The 1660s brought hard times to the Virginia colony. Tobacco
prices were very low and suffering was widespread. Virginia
farmers demanded a one-year moratorium on tobacco production to drive the price up. In this time of hardship, a group of
Gloucester County servants met, during warm summer nights,
at "Mr. Knight's little house in ye woods," a tavern used by the
laboring classes of both races.

These servants were hatching a plot that amounted to the
social revolution America never had. After a month of discussion, nine of them entered into a pact to collect weapons and
recruit allies—"company and arms such as they could gather"
—to meet at an appointed place, and then march to the governor in Jamestown and demand freedom for the servants and
slaves.

The army of revolt was to meet at a place called "the
poplar springs" on Sunday, September 13, 1663. They would
then proceed from house to house across the countryside, seiz-
ing more weapons and recruiting more soldiers from among
the plantation servants and slaves.

On the Saturday night before the appointed day, the nine
conspirators "shooke hands and swore surely to their designes."
They went back to their masters and prepared for revolt. But
they were betrayed. A servant named Birkenhead heard of the
plans and informed his master. The nine were arrested, and the
four deemed most responsible for the plot were hanged.

The potential uprising of servants and slaves represented a
very real and present danger to the established order in the
Virginia colony. This is clear from the fact that the informer,

Birkenhead, was rewarded with his freedom and the incredible sum of 5,000 pounds of tobacco. In addition, the Virginia legislature passed a resolution holding that September 13 should hereafter be marked as a holy day of thanksgiving that the revolt had been averted. The legislature was, of course, made up entirely of men whose prosperity depended upon the use of captive labor.

A real revolt finally came in 1676 when one of the colonial governor's inner circle, a young planter named Nathaniel Bacon, put himself forward as the leader of the poor and oppressed. But Bacon's chosen constituency was not the servants and slaves; instead he represented the small landowners. Much of Bacon's discontent, and that of the inland freeholders, was prompted by the governor's failure to be vicious enough in suppressing the native people of the colony. When Bacon finally took up arms, his army first waged indiscriminate slaughter against the Indians.

Mixed in with the impulse to remove the "Indian threat" there was also a legitimate resentment at the hardening inequalities and corruptions of the colonial social order. As Bacon put it, "The poverty of the country is such that all the power and sway is got into the hands of the rich who . . . having the common people in their debt have always curbed and oppressed them." Bacon also indicted "great men in authority" as "spounges [who] have suckt up the publique treasures [and] juggling parasites whose tottering fortunes have been repaired and supported at the publique charge."

Bacon's uprising enjoyed startling success. While some of his troops pursued the unfortunate Indians to the west, Bacon himself drove the governor out of Jamestown and took control of the colony. Eventually the governor, supported by the arrival of 1,000 troops from Britain, went after Bacon's army. The rebel war then turned away from the Indians and toward protracted battle with the loyalist elite. In this phase of the uprising, needing more troops, Bacon proclaimed freedom for all servants and slaves who joined his army.

The governor had earlier attempted this gambit during his flight from Jamestown, to no avail. But servants and slaves flocked to Bacon's rebel cause and made it their own. For several weeks in the summer of 1676 a bi-racial army of servants, slaves, and poor white farmers ranged up and down the Tidewater plundering the homes of loyalist planters. Bacon may have started his rebel army to fight the Indians, but the servants and slaves joined it to fight for justice and for freedom.

Bacon himself fell ill and died during this phase of the struggle. His army was soon overcome by the superior firepower of the British. At the end of the revolt an English gunship commanded by Captain Thomas Grantham made its way up the York River and reached the central garrison of the rebel forces. There Grantham faced about 400 armed Virginians, English and African alike. Under the threat of Grantham's cannons, and cajoled by false promises of pardon and freedom, most of them surrendered their arms and came aboard. The last holdouts were a group of about eighty blacks and twenty whites, together, who finally surrendered when their ammunition was exhausted.

As these few episodes indicate, at the beginning of the American experiment ordinary black and white people acted more as human beings than as racial categories. They were all, black and white alike, strangers uprooted from their homes and brought together on a new and bewildering continent. As servants or slaves the bulk of them shared the same work, the same quarters, and the same conditions. They found fellowship in spirit and flesh, and they acted together in the mutual interest of their own freedom and dignity.

The servants and slaves partied and worshiped and rebelled together. They formed bonds of affection and shared love. In the surviving records from the 1600s we learn of several cases of interracial marriage. These relationships are simply noted and not remarked upon as the occasion of any scandal.

The first Africans arrived in Virginia in 1619 and their number grew slowly. By 1650 there were still fewer than 500 of them. Throughout the seventeenth century the status of these Africans was in a state of evolution and flux. Most of them had come to Virginia as slaves. Some were free, or became free after a term of service. All of them—slave, free or servant— held a much higher status than that of black slaves in the nineteenth century.

Black slaves and servants in the 1600s were subject to the same punishments as white servants. They could work for money and buy their freedom. They kept and sold their own livestock. In at least one documented case, in 1646, a court made the sale of a slave by his owner contingent upon the slave's consent. Africans freed from slavery or servitude in seventeenth-century Virginia became full members of the community. Racial prejudice undoubtedly existed, but there is little evidence of systematic discrimination.

To scan the minutes of the Virginia legislature from this era is to see an official body wrestling, over several generations, with questions that would come to haunt us all through the centuries. The Virginia colony was built from the start on the necessity of captive labor, whether from white servants or black slaves. A body of law (the "servant codes") was developed very early in the colony's history to deal with the special conditions of people held as property. These laws governed the buying and selling of servants, the punishment of servants, and, especially, the return of runaway servants. Slowly, over the course of a century, the servant codes were converted to a race code governing the institution of black slavery.

Over the course of that formative century we can see economics, ideology, and custom clashing as the colonial order attempted to accommodate the new African arrivals. At first blacks were defined by religion. They were either "heathens" or Christians. If they were Christians they were under the same law as their white counterparts; if "heathen" they were classified with the Indians. Then the prohibition against holding a Christian in lifetime bondage was repealed at the insistence of slave owners.

Alongside this evolution, it also became evident to Virginia's elite that there were serious problems inherent in the system of indentured servanthood. White servants couldn't be held in perpetuity, but they also couldn't be shipped back to England when their term of service was done. England didn't want them; that's why they had come to Virginia. As a result, with the passing of the decades, the number of free, poor whites in Virginia proliferated. They became restless and posed a social problem for the "big men" of the colony.

The first response of the planters to the poor white problem was to lengthen the standard terms of indentured servitude from four to seven years, or until age twenty-four, whichever was longest. Harsher penalties were enacted for fugitive servants. Previously the penalty had been double service. In 1670 it became double service plus four months for every 200 pounds of tobacco spent to capture the runaway. Courts began adding more time to the terms of runaways to compensate for crop loss incurred by the servant's absence from the plantation. Servants could be bound for an additional two years for bearing or fathering an illegitimate child.

These measures contributed to the atmosphere of rebellion among Virginia servants in the 1660s and 1670s, but they could only postpone the inevitable. All the white servants would still eventually be freed, and the poor white sector of society would continue to grow. In the wake of Bacon's Rebellion the specter was raised that the large class of the free-but-poor might make common cause with the other groups at the bottom—the slaves and the servants—with disastrous consequences for the landed gentry.

The threat of such an alliance forced a fundamental rethinking of social policy in Virginia. At the turn of the century the conditions of black slavery grew more rigid. In 1691 a law was passed against miscegenation. Blacks came increasingly to occupy a cordoned-off "other" zone of society. Meanwhile, reforms were made to ameliorate the conditions of the poor whites. In 1705 a new law required that all freed servants be provided with ten bushels of corn, thirty shillings, a gun, and fifty acres of land. Freed white servants were increasingly replaced by black slaves, and the lower classes of whites were drawn into a web of white racial solidarity that induced them to see the "big men" as allies and protectors.

That was the outcome in old Virginia, and there a pattern was established which would be repeated in the South, and throughout the new nation, for the next three centuries. The categories of black and white, as we now know them, were created out of a struggle over the terms by which wealth and power would be allocated in the New World. The racial categories were codified and enshrined so that the relatively poor and powerless majority could be divided. The powerless groups were set apart from one another so that they could be set against each other.

In the process, the land that would become America gained a measure of stability and even achieved a measure of self-rule and democracy for whites. But the achievement came at the cost of horrible violence against blacks and a tragic lowering of horizons and limiting of aspirations for ordinary whites. Lost in the bargain was the opportunity to build a multiracial cooperative commonwealth—something that would have truly been a New World.

This outcome is well known to the casual student of history. But too often we leap straight to the outcome of these founding struggles without pausing to consider the alternatives. In the seventeenth century there truly were alternatives. The fabled racism of America's poor and working-class whites was not, and is not, a natural phenomenon written in the stars. It is the result of a particular set of events and historical forces. It is, at root, a socially constructed fact, not a psychological or theological one. It emerged from the historical process we have just seen, in which the early planter aristocracy consolidated its rule.

The point is that things could have been different. At the beginning black and white Americans ignored the outward signs of racial difference and acted on the clear perception of their common self-interest and their common humanity. In the next three hundred years they, on occasion, did so again. And they still could.

In old Virginia the common bonds between black and white laborers were so self-evident that they could be obscured only by the force of law and the lash. But even under those pressures the common bonds continued to assert themselves, even during the worst days of Southern slavery.

It is a perversely instructive fact of history that the most brutal years of the slave system were the last ones. The turn for the worse came with a vengeance after the 1830 rebellion led by the great Virginia slave preacher, Nat Turner. By the time of Turner's revolt, black slaves far outnumbered whites in much of the South. The prospect of a violent revolt by this huge mass of the oppressed threw a cold terror into the hearts of the slave-owners. They turned that terror back upon their chattel and an inhumane system increasingly became a simply inhuman one.

This change occurred both at the "micro" level, where individual planters made decisions about living conditions and punishments, and at the "macro" level, where pro-slavery forces took a more combative and unyielding stance in national politics, particularly around the issues of the return of fugitives and the expansion of slavery in the West.

At the same time, the nature of the slave system changed with the closing of the slave trade from West Africa. No new slaves could be brought into the country, but the demand for slaves continued to grow in the newly settled Deep South states of Georgia, Alabama, Mississippi, and Louisiana. This was especially true after the invention of the cotton gin made mass production of cotton in the Deep South a profitable concern.

In this context the old Southern states of Virginia and Kentucky became the source for the slave trade. More and more slaves from the upper South were shipped down the river to the newer states. This entailed the cruel separation of black families on a massive scale, a tragedy that took place near the border under the watchful eyes of horrified Northerners. These witnesses included, for instance, the evangelical Beechers of Cincinnati and their literary relative, Harriet Beecher Stowe, who placed the Kentucky-Louisiana slave trade at the center of her novel, *Uncle Tom's Cabin.*

New abolitionist pressures from the North only fanned the flames of slave state extremism. In the South the 1840s and 1850s brought a "circle-the-wagons" wartime mentality. The prospects for white Southern dissent and peaceful change became increasingly untenable. Yet it was during this terrible time that the most significant white Southern movement against slavery arose.

# Chapter 3

# A Sign of Contradiction

*Kentucky Abolitionists in the Antebellum South*

## Rebel for a Free South

William Shreve Bailey was a journeyman mechanic in northern Kentucky in the 1830s. In 1839 he opened his own machine shop in the Ohio River town of Newport. Bailey was the father of ten children. He was a man who sweated and strove to feed those children and to achieve the measure of self-determination that came with owning a business.

But Bailey was also a man who could not limit his horizons to the pursuit of personal success. He was a mechanic who also read widely and thought his own thoughts. When the great debate about slavery heated up in the 1840s William Shreve Bailey was listening. He followed the controversy in the press. He looked at the slave society around him and considered the arguments about the morality of slavery. In Newport it was impossible not to hear these, with voluble abolitionists working just across the river in Cincinnati.

From the clamor and grease of his machine shop Bailey heard the arguments for and against the peculiar institution, but he also found himself thinking about the social position of white workingmen like himself. He wondered what benefit free wage workers gained from having to compete with slave labor. He wondered who in Kentucky would really be hurt by the abolition of slavery and who might be helped.

From his own thought and study, William Shreve Bailey reached the conclusion that human slavery was, in fact, morally wrong. This in itself was no revolution. Many advocates for Southern slave society admitted that slavery was an evil but, they argued, it was a necessary evil, or at least one that, for practical reasons, could not be eliminated in the foreseeable future.

But Bailey did not stop with a moral judgment about slavery. He also decided that slavery was an obstacle to the well-being and social progress of the non-slaveholding white Southern majority. No workingman, he realized, could reap the full value from his labor so long as some workers were held in absolute bondage. Especially in the emerging non-agricultural labor market of Southern towns and cities, progress for any one worker required progress for all.

From this rich stew of social ferment, amid the demands of physical labor and the pressures of a large and growing household, mechanic William Shreve Bailey of Newport, Kentucky became, against all odds and expectations, an abolitionist. He was not a gradual emancipationist. That was the position held in those days by a minority of respectable Kentucky ministers and politicians. Instead Bailey began to advocate the immediate and total abolition of slavery. He demanded nothing less than the conversion of the Southern economy into a free and biracial wage labor market.

As these thoughts took shape and solidified in Bailey's mind, Bailey looked to give them public voice. So, in the grand tradition of grassroots American rebels and reformers, Bailey inked up his pen and put his ideas on paper. Then he sent them off to the editor of his local newspaper, the *Newport News*.

Bailey's first letter to the editor was published, and widely condemned on the streets of Newport. But Bailey was not deterred by criticism. He initiated a steady stream of opinionated articles answering his critics and advancing his views. He became practiced in debate and argumentation and grew to love the rhetorical battlefield. The more controversy swirled around him, the more Bailey became convinced of his social mission.

Meanwhile the editor of the small town *Newport News* was bewildered. He felt obliged to print Bailey's missives. They were news. The Southern abolitionist mechanic was a man-bites-dog story if he'd ever seen one. But Bailey was making news and making enemies, and the editor was getting his share of both. The editor wasn't in the newspaper business to make enemies, he was in it to make money. He didn't want to shut down Bailey's crusade, but he didn't want to be hostage to it, either.

Eighteen-fifty was the year of the debate on the Fugitive Slave Act, which made it a crime to assist escaping slaves, even in the North. Bailey's arguments against that law were especially volatile, and the pro-slavery harassment directed at the *Newport News* grew especially intense. At last the *News* editor came to Bailey with a suggestion: Perhaps the abolitionist would be interested in selling his machine shop and buying a printing press? William Shreve Bailey scraped up $650 to buy the *Newport News* and never looked back.

Under Bailey's proprietorship, the *Newport News* became an abolitionist organ with the blood-stirring and evocative title, the *Free South*. Running an abolitionist paper in a Southern slave state was not an occupation for the faint of heart. Trouble came early, in October 1851, when an angry mob of pro-slavery whites burned the building that housed Bailey's press. Of course most of the advertisers who had supported the *Newport News* boycotted the *Free South*.

But Bailey still made a go of the paper by enlisting his large brood of children as typesetters. The paper continued to appear and to provide a clear and forthright voice of Southern working-class dissent in the slavery debate that raged throughout the 1850s. From his peculiar vantage point, Bailey opposed the westward spread of slavery and the Dred Scott decision of the Supreme Court which upheld the Fugitive Slave Act. In issue after issue Bailey hammered away at his argument that abolition was in the economic interest of the great majority of Southern workers and farmers.

When the Republican Party was founded in 1854 to oppose the spread of slavery, Bailey made it his political home. He also looked to Northern abolitionists for financial assistance to keep his paper afloat. Some donations did come his way from Northern sympathizers, but one attempt to enlist institutional support for his work met with an especially telling rejection.

The American Missionary Association (AMA) was the umbrella organization for support of evangelical Christian abolitionist activities throughout the Midwestern states. The AMA agent for Kentucky was a young Bracken County Presbyterian minister named John Fee. On behalf of the AMA, Fee was sent to Newport to evaluate William Bailey's work and to make a recommendation about funding.

Fee wrote a negative report, noting that Bailey did not promote the full radical abolitionist agenda in sufficiently moralistic terms and that there was little religious cast to the work of the *Free South*. Bailey was rejected by the abolitionists because he used economic arguments that appealed to the self-interest of the white working class instead of pietistic arguments that appealed solely to the conscience.

The lack of funds, however, did not silence the *Free South*. The tragic final chapter for the paper did not come until late in 1859. On October 22 of that year John Brown staged his famous raid on the U.S. Army arsenal at Harper's Ferry, Virginia (now West Virginia). Brown's threat to arm the slave population created an even greater panic among white Southerners than had the Nat Turner rebellion. All antislavery activity was identified with Brown's violent fanaticism.

On October 28 an angry mob attacked Bailey's offices, moved his printing press out into the street, and strewed most of the type (the metal letters used for printing) into the gutter. The next night another raiding party seized a clutch of original manuscripts from the office. Bailey was warned to leave the state or face worse violence.

Instead, he filed suit against the men responsible for the damage to his business and swore that he would only leave Kentucky "... dead and some of them at least must die with me." Bailey solicited money from Northern supporters and re-established his press. But when he resumed publication of the *Free South* he was immediately arrested for "incendiary writings." Northern abolitionists bailed him out and sent him on an extended fundraising trip to England. By the time Bailey returned, the controversy had been rendered moot by the onset of the Civil War.

### The True American and the Art of the Possible

The pretentious polysyllabic moniker of "Cassius Marcellus Clay" is a name with a history. Today that name is most widely known as the one given at birth to the great heavyweight boxing champion Muhammad Ali. Clay was the "slave name" that Ali shed when he became a Muslim in 1964.

Under his Arabic title, Ali went on to become, for a while, the most famous man on earth. But Ali, when he was still Clay, was a native of Louisville, Kentucky. And in Kentucky Cassius M. Clay is a name that signifies mightily in the complexities of America's racial history.

Clay was a slaveholder who tried to end slavery. He was an aristocrat who wanted to serve the interests of the common people. Cassius Marcellus Clay was a relative of "The Great Compromiser," former Speaker of the U.S. House of Representatives, Henry Clay. And Cassius M. Clay, too, was a politician with undisguised ambitions for state and national office. But he was also a visionary who sought to create and then represent a constituency that did not yet exist and for the most part did not even know its own name.

Clay was the antislavery figure who made it possible for a William Shreve Bailey to arise. Clay was the public figure, the "great man" of his region, who extended protection to other, more radical, Kentucky abolitionists. All the while he sought to hedge his position and protect his political viability, though in the end he won no office higher than state representative.

In his day Cassius Marcellus Clay was known as "The Lion of Whitehall." Whitehall was the estate he built in Madison

County, near Richmond, at the edge of the central Kentucky Bluegrass. The two-story brick mansion at Whitehall still stands. It is a tourist attraction in Richmond. It is advertised as an antebellum period piece, a nostalgia trip into the Old South, to rival "The Old Kentucky Home" plantation house in nearby Bardstown.

Early nineteenth-century Kentucky was not *Gone With the Wind*. Clay was an antebellum aristocrat. He was born into wealth and educated at Yale. But he was a hard-drinking, cussing, tobacco-chewing, pistol-dueling frontier aristocrat. Clay was born in 1810. He was the son of General Green Clay, one of the wealthiest slaveholders in the entire state of Kentucky.

As a student in New Haven Cassius Clay heard the great abolitionist, William Lloyd Garrison speak. He later recalled that Garrison's speech "...was a new revelation to me....I then resolved," Clay wrote, "that when I had the strength, if ever, I would give slavery a death struggle."

When the young Clay returned to the South he began a political career almost at once, but his antislavery conversion was in dormant gestation. Clay was elected to the Kentucky legislature in 1835 as a Whig, but not as an abolitionist.

By 1840 he was calling himself an emancipationist. Clay put forward a plan that would phase out slavery by declaring, some decades in advance, that every female slave born after a designated date would be free. Every child held the status of its mother, so with the passing of a generation, slavery would finally end. In various incarnations the emancipationist proposal used target dates ranging all the way from 1860 to 1900.

In 1840, when he came out as an antislavery advocate, Clay said, "I believe slavery to be an evil—an evil morally, economically, physically, intellectually, socially, religiously, politically ...an unmixed evil." But he rarely emphasized the moral, humanitarian, or religious arguments against slavery. At around the same time he also said, "It [the slavery question] is not a matter of conscience with me [and] I press it not upon the consciences of others."

Instead, Clay argued that slavery was an economic disaster for non-slaveholders. He pointed to the glaring disparities of economic development and prosperity that existed between the neighboring states of Kentucky and Ohio. He urged Southern working-class whites to look to their own interests rather than be drawn into a false racial alliance with the slaveholders.

Clay sought to stake out a creative new position in the political scene, one that was simultaneously principled, realistic, and progressive. In the short run his efforts were all for naught. His new ideas were rejected and Clay lost his seat in the legislature in the election of 1841.

While Clay encountered resistance from his white neighbors in promoting an end to slavery, he also had difficulty gaining support from the traditional antislavery forces in the North. One glaring problem which the abolitionists could not overlook was the simple fact that Cassius Clay was himself still a slaveowner. Thirteen years after he came of legal age, and for a full four years after he declared himself a public enemy of the institution, Clay still held human beings as property on his Madison County plantation.

Finally in 1844 he freed all of his slaves, and spent some $100,000 to buy the freedom of their separated family members. But even then he did keep on his plantation a few slaves who were not his personal chattel but the property of the family estate, and so, he claimed, outside of his control. This remained a nagging issue between Clay and his abolitionist brethren throughout his public life.

Turned out of public office, and not content with the life of a gentleman farmer, in January 1845 Clay established an emancipationist newspaper, called the *True American*, in Lexington. The paper promoted his ideas about the economic costs of slavery and the drain it imposed upon the non-slaveholding whites.

The *True American* was controversial from the start. But Clay's first real trouble came in August 1845. That was when Clay published an editorial written from his sickbed while he was suffering from a very high fever. The article addressed the slaveholders of Kentucky, stating, "But remember, you who dwell in marble palaces, that there are strong arms and fiery hearts and iron pikes in the streets, and pains [sic] of glass only between them and the silver plate on board and the smooth-skinned woman on the ottoman. When you have mocked at virtue, denied the agency of God in the affairs of men, and made rapine your honeyed faith, tremble! For the day of retribution is at hand, and the masses will be avenged!"

However ill he was, Clay could not have been more fevered than this stretch of prose which seemed calculated to push every hot button in the white racial psyche. Its fantasy of violent sexual revenge could have been written perhaps only by a guilt-ridden slaveholder, like Clay, at a time when his defenses were down. Clay's white readers did not miss a single connotation or subtext in his editorial and they rose as a mob against him.

Clay eventually repudiated the article and admitted that his illness had "almost incessantly" affected his brain, but he stood by antislavery convictions, and, for the mob, the apology was too little, too late. A city judge issued an order for the *True American* to cease publication. The press was seized by a vigilante delegation and shipped to Cincinnati.

When Clay's big trouble came, white Northern abolitionists were silent. They were never comfortable with Clay's homegrown "emancipationism." They were suspicious, in roughly equal parts, of his relaxed code of personal and political ethics, his frontier style, and his appeals to lower-class white self-interest.

Interestingly enough, in 1845, among the famous abolitionists of the day, only Frederick Douglass rallied to Cassius Clay's side. Douglass called the *True American* "a star shining in the darkness, beaming hope to the almost despairing bondsman."

Clay eventually reopened the Lexington office of the *True American* and resumed publication. But, for insurance, he kept the printing plant permanently headquartered across the Ohio and ferried the copy back and forth. Clay stepped back into the political arena in 1851 when he ran for governor as the candidate of the "Emancipation Party." He was soundly defeated again, but he ran fairly well in the hill and mountain country of eastern Kentucky, just to the east and south of his Richmond home.

After the election Clay began to concentrate his political efforts on cultivating an antislavery base in this upland country. In Kentucky's Cumberland and Allegheny mountains there were few slaves. The white population lived by subsistence farming on the small plots of cultivable land. Here, among the white yeoman farmers, Clay thought that he saw a natural constituency for his economic campaign against slavery.

The hill people, Clay hoped, could become the core of a native Southern white constituency that would act on its interests against the plantation aristocracy and so act as a wedge to break open the slave society. In so doing, the yeoman whites could do good for themselves, for the Commonwealth, for the blacks in bondage and, at the same time, do wonders for Cassius Clay's frustrated political ambitions.

The mountain people were of a fiercely independent spirit, and they were intensely devoted to their revivalist religion. So it happened that in the 1850s, as the slavery controversy rattled toward its bloody and explosive climax, Cassius Clay entered into an alliance with a stiff-necked and puritanical Southern abolitionist revival preacher.

## The City on a Ridge

John Fee was the abolitionist preacher who rejected William Shreve Bailey's work as insufficiently principled and so undeserving of funding by the Northern evangelicals. Fee was born in Bracken County, Kentucky, along the Ohio River, east of Cincinnati, in 1816. He grew up in a slaveholding family of strong Presbyterians and in 1842 Fee entered Lane Theological Seminary in Cincinnati to study for the ministry.

At Lane he experienced what he perceived as a dramatic religious conversion. He became convinced of the great evil of slavery. He later reported that he knelt alone and prayed,

"Lord, if needs be, make me an Abolitionist." A short time later, Fee felt the call to go home to Kentucky and take up the fight against slavery there. This call was hastened when the elder Mr. Fee, having learned of his son's new enthusiasm, cut off his money supply.

At that point, Fee left Lane Seminary and returned home as a genuine fire-and-brimstone Christian evangelical abolitionist. He came back preaching that a true Christian conversion would show fruit in an abolitionist commitment, and, conversely, that slaveholders should be excluded from Christian fellowship. Fee's abolitionism did not calculate economic interests or test the political winds. He wrote, "In whatever way we enter our protest against slavery it must be for the good reason that it is sin against God." This was not a view that blended easily with the accommodation of local realities and self-interest politics as practiced by Clay or the other "emancipationists" who could have been Fee's allies.

In keeping with his principles, Fee refused calls to pastor several churches that wanted him to ignore, or play down, the slavery issue. Finally he accepted the pastorate of a tiny congregation at Cabin Creek in Lewis County, also in eastern Kentucky. When Fee arrived at Cabin Creek, the church had five members. Two of them soon resigned.

Fee insisted that there would be no slaveholders in his congregation, ever, regardless of their professions of faith. Eventually the Presbyterian Synod dismissed him from the denomination for this stand. By the time he was dismissed, however, Fee had built up a small following of parishioners who joined him in a new, non-denominational "Church of Christ."

Around this time Fee also won the support of the American Missionary Association and became its Kentucky representative. By the early 1850s Fee's Cabin Creek church had thirty-five full members and drew one hundred Sunday worshippers. Another church he served in Bracken County was even larger, and both congregations had voted to admit blacks as equal members.

Fee also conducted abolitionist preaching campaigns elsewhere in the state. He rode the circuit on horseback, visiting any church that would have him. An 1854 preaching mission in Madison County happened to coincide with Cassius Clay's new interest in cultivating a hill country constituency. Clay was impressed with the young preacher and his message, and with the crowds he drew. He urged him to come back to Madison County and start an antislavery church, with a residential community around it that could serve as a living model for a free labor society and a training center for the antislavery cause.

Clay backed this proposal with financial support and also donated ten acres of land, on a ridge at the very foot of the Cumberland Mountains, to start the community. Fee accepted the offer and brought his family to Madison County. He named their new ridgetop home Berea, after the town mentioned in the book of Acts where the gospel was received "with open hearts."

The Berea church community began winning adherents quickly. But it won even more enemies. In 1855 Fee had his first brush with violence when, in the neighboring town of Crab Orchard, a mob of angry whites pulled him from the church where he was preaching and dumped him at the edge of town. After this incident, Cassius Clay offered an armed guard for Fee's next speaking engagement. When the preacher rejected this offer, Clay instead extended to Fee the protection of his prestige as a "great man" of the area. He did this by personally accompanying Fee on the podium at his next public speech in Rockcastle County.

But the uneasy alliance of the pacifist preacher and the pistol-wielding politician was bound to be a troubled one. A decisive break came on July 4, 1856 when Fee, with Clay behind him waiting to take the podium, delivered a ringing condemnation of the Fugitive Slave Act. He promised to disobey the law and insisted that "a law confessedly contrary to the law of God ought not by human courts be enforced."

Clay, in his subsequent remarks, warned the crowd that Fee's exhortation was illegal and dangerous. Good citizens were bound to obey the law of the land, like it or not, he said. This sent a signal through the region that Clay's protection of the Bereans was weakening. The weakness was quickly exploited and a steady campaign of harassment against the abolitionist colony began. One of Fee's daughters later recalled, "When I was little I thought everyone had mobs. They were as inevitable as the weather. We thought nothing more about mobs than most people do about thunderstorms."

In spite of these troubles, however, Fee and his followers did manage to open Berea College in 1858, and the Berea Church continued to gain new converts. As it did for William Bailey, disaster for the Berea community came in October 1859, with the John Brown raid at Harper's Ferry.

As it happened, the raid occurred while John Fee was on a fundraising tour in the North. Shortly after the raid Fee was preaching at Henry Ward Beecher's church in Brooklyn, New York when he said these words: "We want more John Browns, not in manner of action but in spirit of consecration; not to go with carnal weapons, but with spiritual; men who, with Bibles in their hands, and tears in their eyes, will beseech man to be reconciled to God. Give us such men, and we may yet save the South."

Of course, the New York press reported this statement. And, inevitably, by the time word of the speech reached Kentucky, and was published in the *Louisville Daily Courier,* the report had Fee saying only that "More John Browns were wanted, especially for Kentucky."

In Kentucky this was interpreted as an open call for armed slave revolts. As a result of this supposed statement, wild rumors flew about the goings-on at Berea. Trainloads of Northerners with large suspicious trunks were supposed to be converging on the settlement. A Berea-bound shipment suspected of containing weapons was seized by the authorities and broken open, only to expose a collection of dangerous candle molds.

In written statements dispatched from the North, Fee tried to correct the falsification of his views. But in the passion of the moment reason was futile. After all, he did have to confess to the fateful words, "We want more John Browns." In the atmosphere that prevailed in the South in those days that was all that counted.

In Fee's absence, George Rogers, an AMA missionary, was the leader of the Berea community. A mob of sixty armed men arrived at his house one night claiming to represent the citizens of Madison County. The mob ordered Rogers, his family, and the entire Berea colony to leave the state. The Bereans appealed to the state courts and to the governor, but to no avail. Finally, at the end of the year, thirty-two Bereans departed in wagons, winding up cold, muddy roads north toward Cincinnati. Fee eventually joined them there.

On January 10, 1860 Cassius Clay came to the abolitionists' defense one last time. For three hours he stood on the steps of the state capitol at Frankfort, in a cold, driving rain, and spoke to a crowd of several hundred in defense of Fee, the Bereans, and the right of free speech in Kentucky. "There were not a better people in the state," he said, "than those surrounding the colony at Berea." But by the time Clay raised his voice the first group of Bereans was already in exile. In the next few months sixty more people would be driven from their homes in the city on a ridge.

John Fee and his family returned to Berea in 1864, as the Civil War was winding down. The area around Madison County was securely under Union control. In the fall of 1864 Berea College reopened. In the same year, at nearby Camp Nelson, Fee had the opportunity for the first time to preach to a large group of Negro soldiers. It was an intensely moving experience for him, and in it he saw the germ of a postwar mission to provide educational and religious training for the blacks of Kentucky who would soon be freed en masse.

And so in 1866 the postwar history of Berea College began. For thirty-eight years the school thrived as a biracial institute offering higher education to the children of slavery and the poor white children of the mountains, side by side. In 1878 a president of Berea College was able to say with pride that "not less than 100 Negro schools were taught last year by colored teachers educated at Berea."

Through most of those postwar years the student body at Berea was roughly half black and half white. No distinctions of color were drawn in any of the school's activities. As a later president of the college wrote, "It is no unimportant part of a white boy's education for him to see the Negro treated as a man."

This grand experiment in interracial, working-class education in the Southern mountains ended at the turn of the century, but only after it was specifically outlawed by an act of the Kentucky legislature. In the 1890s segregation laws were being adopted all over the South and Kentucky was no exception. Integration in all public schools and public places was banned before the end of the century. But Berea continued on as an efficient and appealing sign of contradiction in the early days of the Jim Crow era.

Finally, another act was passed in 1904, the Day Act, which specifically prohibited racial integration in *private* schools. When this law came down, Berea's trustees set aside a proportionate share of the school's endowment to begin Lincoln College for blacks in Louisville.

Berea then concentrated on a mission to the impoverished and uneducated in Appalachia, who were, by demographic fact, almost all white. In 1950 the Day Act was repealed and Berea resumed its tradition of interracial cooperation, just in time to serve as a beacon of new, and old, possibilities during the turbulent years of the civil rights movement.

## The Success of a Failure

To Americans who are familiar only with the soundbite version of our history, the very existence of the Kentucky antislavery movement is a powerful sign of contradiction. Of course the white antislavery Kentuckians, of all ideological stripes, ultimately failed. Only war ended chattel bondage in America.

But for anyone prone to stereotypes about the racial attitudes of Southerners, or working-class whites in general, the inconvenient fact remains that, even among the whites of a Southern slave state, there were important voices speaking out for freedom and equality. And those voices included people who benefited directly from the slave system (the slaveowner Clay) and people who were most subjected to the racial propaganda of the slave system (Bailey, the working-class white). It is also noteworthy that the state of Kentucky also produced from its own soil at least one genuine, barn-burning, pure abolitionist zealot in the person of John Fee.

Beyond revealing the obvious fact that human beings are unpredictable animals, the linked stories of William Shreve Bailey, Cassius Clay, and John Fee also open up a rich field of questions about class and race consciousness, moralism and self-interest, and cultural accommodation and radical witness. Ultimately, the greatest significance to be gleaned from the Kentucky stories, however, is the ongoing fact of Berea College's existence.

That remarkable institution stands today precisely because it has in its history combined the regionally rooted class instincts of William Bailey and the moral vision and iron integrity of John Fee. And only the protection of the accommodationist, Clay, got it through the most vulnerable years of infancy. In the decades after the Civil War, Berea represented an important biracial working-class experiment. Since reintegrating in the 1950s, the school has remained mostly white simply because of the demographics of Appalachia. But the vision of a Free South, founded on the cooperation and unity of black and white working people, remains at the core of the college's vision and witness.

The same political trend of the 1890s that ended integrated education at Berea College was in force throughout the South. The arrival of Jim Crow on the Southern, and American, scene came in response to the threat posed by the populist uprising. This was a late nineteenth-century political movement of workers and farmers that arose, especially in the West and South, to challenge the power of the new Eastern industrial and financial elite. It was a movement to forge an economic democracy out of the new national political democracy created by the Civil War.

In many parts of the South, the populist movement made interracial working-class unity its most powerful tool against the economic and political power of the planter elites. In the 1880s and 1890s Southern blacks could still vote, and did in large numbers. When they voted along lines of economic interest and in alliance with lower-class whites, the two groups formed huge popular majorities almost everywhere in the region.

Populists in the Midwest, the West, and the South sought to free rural and small-town America from the domination of outside financial and industrial interests. The South was crucial for making this movement into a national majority coalition. The populists hoped to return the destiny of the country to the hands of the people who dug its dirt, and in the South those working hands were black and white in roughly equal numbers. Together, it seemed, they could shake the very foundations of American economic power.

CHAPTER 4

# "Separately Fleeced"

*The Populist Rebellion and the
Lost Hope of Reconstruction*

### In the Ditch Together

In late October, 1892 a man set out on horseback from the Hickory Hill plantation into the countryside around Thomson, Georgia, west of Augusta. Like Paul Revere, the rider passed from farmhouse to tenant shack issuing a call to arms. One of their number was in danger and in need of protection. Throughout south Georgia white men came out of those poor houses, with guns. They mounted their horses or wagons and rode toward the appointed spot. Along the way they spread the word to other men, and they picked up their guns and rode away, too.

Hundreds of armed white men rode all night on the dirt roads of McDuffie County. They came on horseback and in farm wagons. They rode until the horses staggered from exhaustion. All through the night, and for the whole next day, they poured into the little village of Thomson, and onto the grounds of Tom Watson's farm at Hickory Hill. When darkness came again, the farmers' army was at least 2,000 strong. The streets of Thomson village were lined with wagons and exhausted animals and all human attention was focused on the confrontation that loomed out at the Watson place.

Hickory Hill was a fair-sized estate. The main house, though not quite a mansion, was large, with two stories and two fireplaces, and a broad and deep front porch with classic Greek columns. In the middle of the long walkway leading up to the house there was a fountain rising from the center of a large circular reflecting pool.

For three long days and nights in late October, rough, unshaven men in slouch hats, overalls, and worn denim coats sat on the wall of the fountain, keeping watch, with long-barreled guns balanced across their knees. During those days and nights rifles and shotguns were stacked high, like firewood, across the fine front porch of the Watson home. Alongside the pile of weapons were dozens of wooden crates of ammunition. The men were there to defend one of their political spokesmen against a threatened mob assault.

The white men who comprised this ad hoc militia were members of the Farmers' Alliance and supporters of the new populist People's Party. Some of them were small landowners, some of them were tenants or sharecroppers. All of them were poor men. The Southern economy had never really recovered from the destruction of the Civil War. The "Gilded Age" of big banking and railroad trusts meant nothing for the rural South but hard credit and low crop prices. When poverty reached hunger, the farmers rebelled.

The poor white folks looked to Tom Watson as their leader, in Georgia and all over the South. He represented them in Congress, and in 1892 he was in the middle of a brutal re-election campaign. There was violence against populist supporters, and the very real possibility that, no matter how many votes Watson got, the election would be stolen. The bankers and big businessmen of Augusta were so disturbed by the populist threat that they sent a special appeal to the New York tycoons who owned ever-larger chunks of the South. According to the *New York Tribune*, "Insurance and railroad companies responded liberally, so that $40,000 was in hand for use, in addition to the local funds."

Those were the stakes, and the odds. That is why, when Watson sent out an alarm, these men dropped their work and came. But this army of white farmers was not gathered at Hickory Hill to protect Tom Watson himself. They were there to protect Rev. H. S. Doyle, a black man, and a populist.

H. S. Doyle was a Georgia preacher and in 1892 he was still a young man. He was a member of the first generation of African Americans to grow up in America as citizens, not slaves. He was raised in the years of the Reconstruction when Southern blacks—"freedmen," they were called—voted and held public office and educated themselves under the protection of federal troops. But in 1892 the Reconstruction was long over and H. S. Doyle was grown. The federal troops and administrators had returned to their homes in the North, and black and white Southerners were left to themselves to work out the shape of their post-slavery world.

In the fall of 1892, young preacher Doyle did a lot of preaching. Sometimes he preached in church, and sometimes he preached in town halls, or on street corners and courthouse squares, or out in the middle of the south Georgia cotton fields. When he preached he talked about justice and equality and unity. He talked about the hard times in the countryside. He talked about the lynchings of black men that went unpunished. He talked about the convict labor lease system in which prisoners, mostly black, were hired out to private employers to take the place of free workers and hold down wages for black and white workers alike.

But, most of all, in his sermons that fall, H. S. Doyle talked about the low price of cotton and the high cost of living. He talked about who was getting richer and who was getting poorer. He talked about the grand alliance of the big planters down South with the big bankers and railroad men up North.

When his audiences were convinced and ready to fall into his hand, Doyle also talked about a new political party, a "people's party," whose platform said "wealth belongs to him who creates it." He would tell his audience that this was a party for the farmers and workers, for people like them, the majority, regardless of color. This people's party would defend black people's citizenship rights and their economic rights at the same time.

In the fall of 1892, the altar call in these sermons was always the same. An election for Congress was coming, and the people's party man was Tom Watson. In the course of his many orations on behalf of Watson for Congress, Doyle certainly must have quoted these words from his candidate. The People's Party says to the Negro and the white, "You are kept apart that you may be separately fleeced of your earnings. You are made to hate each other because upon that hatred is rested the keystone of the arch of financial despotism which enslaves you both. You are deceived and blinded that you may not see how this race antagonism perpetuates a monetary system which beggars both."

That was the policy of the People's Party. Black and white workers and farmers were "in the ditch together," as a Texas populist put it, and they had to pull together to get out. During that last week of October, as election day drew near, H. S. Doyle received word that a lynch mob was coming to send him into permanent silence. In the atmosphere of the campaign, the threat was credible, so Doyle rode as quickly as he could to Hickory Hill for shelter. Tom Watson took him in, and sent a rider out to gather the populist forces in his defense.

The sheriff of McDuffie County was a populist and he joined the troops at Hickory Hill. On the second day of the stand, the sheriff led the 2,000 men as they marched, under arms, to the courthouse in Thomson. There Doyle and Watson appeared at the top of the courthouse steps to address the troops. "We are determined," Watson said, "that in this free country that humblest white or black man that wants to talk our doctrine shall do it, and the man doesn't live who shall touch a hair of his head, without fighting every man in the People's Party."

The farmers remained at the ready for two more days then, convinced that the danger had passed, they dispersed. The next week, on the eve of the voting, H. S. Doyle was speaking from a platform in Louisville, Georgia when a shot rang out. The bullet, clearly intended for the black preacher, missed. It struck a nearby white man in the back and killed him instead.

## "... Make Us Feel That We Are Men"

The populist movement was hardly a model of racial unity and equality by any standard other than that of the nineteenth-century South. In fact, the main institutional expression of the movement, the Farmer's Alliance, was segregated. The original organization was all white, and it spun off a separate Colored Farmer's Alliance that was more than an auxiliary but less than an equal partner. When the Alliances, along with other allies and sympathizers, consolidated forces in the People's Party, nationally and regionally, the racial question was at the forefront.

In August, 1891, at the party's founding convention in Texas, a white delegate put forward a resolution that would have kept blacks from holding party offices or serving on party committees. A black delegate from Fort Worth quickly took the floor in opposition. He first appealed to the delegates' sense of pragmatism, stating, correctly, that "The Negro vote will be the balancing vote in Texas. If you are going to win," he continued, "you will have to take the Negro with you.... You must appoint us by convention and make us feel that we are men."

A white Alliance leader stood in support to say simply, "The colored people are part of the people, and they must be recognized as such." After a full debate a vote was taken, and the Texas People's Party set out on an integrated footing with two black members elected to the State Executive Committee.

A few months later, in early 1892, delegates from around the country met in St. Louis to establish a national People's Party. At that convention, William Warwick, a black Virginian, was nominated for the post of assistant secretary. A white delegate from Georgia took the floor and moved that the nomination be made unanimous. Thickening his drawl to the limit, the Georgian pronounced, "I wish to say that we can stand that down in Georgia." The vote was taken and support for Warwick was unanimous, except for a lone nay-sayer in the Alabama section.

Later that year, the People's Party met in Omaha to nominate a presidential candidate and adopt a platform. There, in the heart of the heartland, amid oceans of red, white, and blue bunting, a representative sample of rural and small town America adopted a platform which, among other things, declared:

> Wealth belongs to him who creates it, and every dollar taken from industry without an equivalent is robbery.... The interests of rural and civil labor are the same; their enemies are identical.... We believe that the time has come when the railroad corporations will either own the people or the people must own the railroads.... Transportation being a means of exchange and a public necessity, the government should own and operate the railroads in the interest of the people.... The telegraph and telephone, like the post office system, being a necessity for the transmission of news, should be owned and operated by the government in the interest of the people....

Election Day 1892 finally came amid violence and fraud and bizarre ballot-counting arithmetic. A movement which, according to the *Atlanta Constitution*, threatened to bring "anarchy [and] communism" to the South, could have expected little else. Back in Tom Watson's Georgia district, the old-line Democrats won an election that hardly anyone would have called free or fair. Watson contested it through legal channels for the next four years.

As had happened since the end of Reconstruction, many black Southerners did not vote, but were "voted" by white Democratic Party thugs who compelled them to the polls and gave orders on how to mark the ballot. In Augusta, Georgia, one of those thugs, a certain Dan Bowles, was marching a line of fifty black men off to the polls when they encountered a group of populists. Isaac Horton, a black populist, tried to pull one of the black men out of the line. A fight broke out, which ended when Bowles fired a gunshot through Isaac Horton's heart and killed him.

In the same city on the same day a Democratic deputy sheriff named Henry Head charged into the Populist Campaign Club in the working class district of the Fifth Ward. He intended to take into custody Arthur Glover, the Populist secretary for the district. Glover shot the sheriff in the stomach and, as Head lay dying, fled through the woods, across the state line into South Carolina.

The price of dissent was high for the populists, and highest of all for the blacks in the movement. It was estimated that, in Georgia alone, fifteen black people were killed by the opponents of Populism during the 1892 elections. In Rukersville, while a white populist was escorting a mixed group of blacks and whites to the polls, they encountered one B. H. Head and several other Democratic stalwarts. According to the Augusta paper, Head recognized some of the black populists as being people "who had once lived with him and who bore the name of Head" (as slaves, of course). Enraged, Head took up a wooden pole and attacked an old black man with it. The black man's son came back with fists flying. Head ended the disturbance with his shotgun, killing one black man and wounding another.

**What Might Have Been...**

The populist legacy is one of the more controversial subjects in U.S. history. This is especially true of the white populists' stance toward blacks in the South. There is no question that, at least rhetorically, the populists showed a support for black people's rights that was, for the time and place, downright revolutionary. Populist platforms and pronouncements opposed lynching, convict labor leasing, and all attempts to limit black political participation. Looking back at the populist record in his classic book *Tom Watson: Agrarian Rebel* (1938), historian C. Vann Woodward concluded, "Never before or since have the two races in the South come so close together as they did during the Populist struggles."

Later historians have questioned Woodward's claims for the populists. They note that when in office they actually did little to further the interests of black supporters, and that they did nothing to counter the racial segregation practices that were bound to keep blacks in a subordinate social role. According to these historians, the record suggests that the white populists were not really committed to racial equality, never really cared about the concerns of their black neighbors, and were interested in blacks only to the extent that they needed their votes to win power for white candidates.

In this regard, Tom Watson is also an emblematic figure. After the populist defeat in the national elections of 1896, Watson withdrew from politics for several years. During this exile he decided that the interracial populist alliance in the South was doomed to fail. Watson bitterly turned on the past and became the destroyer of his own failed dreams. When he returned to public life, Watson supported disenfranchisement of black voters.

Watson's former allies in the West and North looked on in horror as in the later years of his political career he became known both for his economic radicalism (which never wavered) *and* his vicious bigotry against blacks, Jews, and Catholics. In this phase of his life, Watson was closely identified with the rebirth of the Ku Klux Klan. In *Agrarian Rebel* Woodward writes of this time, "if any mortal man may be credited...with releasing the forces of human malice and ignorance and prejudice, which the Klan merely mobilized, that man was Thomas E. Watson."

The alliance of the black and white poor in the South was a fairly short-lived phenomenon. It began in earnest in 1891 and ended with the dramatic failure of the populist ticket in the elections of 1896. The coffin of class-based politics in the South was sealed by the wave of constitutional conventions that swept the Southern states between 1890 and the first years of the new century. These new state constitutions brought in the measures, mainly the poll tax and the literacy test, which were used to disenfranchise Southern blacks and a large number of poor whites.

But in those five brief years, despite all the odds, something new did enter history. It was not something perfect, but it was something promising. As historical critics have noted, white populists were motivated by self-interest. But so were the black populists. That was the foundation of the alliance. Together the biracial lower class of farmers, tenants, and workers formed a voting majority throughout the South. Apart they did not. So the white farmers and workers supported black human rights in order to keep their black partners voting in the coalition for economic reform. But regardless of motivations, even personal prejudices, blacks still got their human rights from the bargain, as well as a significant amount of leverage on the institutions of power.

And even in the limited ways that it was actually practiced in the 1890s, populist interracial cooperation was not all one-sided. The populist racial record varied from state to state. It was best in Texas, Georgia, and North Carolina and worst in Mississippi and Alabama. Everywhere blacks were recruited to support white candidates at the top of the ticket. But in those states where the commitment to the interracial alliance was clear, the populists also nominated or endorsed black candidates in local races. And some of these were elected. In some locations the populists also pursued a "fusion" strategy of running joint tickets with the black-dominated Republican Party.

When we look back at the history of the 1890s we know all too well what happened after the populists lost. It is harder for us to imagine what might have happened if they had won. Foreknowledge of the outcome makes it difficult to recapture the immense possibilities that were contained in that moment. But the fact remains that in those years the possibility of a very different America was there, on the ground, in flesh and blood, and in motion. However haltingly and imperfectly, a new social contract on race and class was being worked out in the lives of the nation's poorest and most powerless people. It was a covenant grounded in shared economic and political interests and a shared commitment to democratic ideals.

In her classic essay, "Ideology and Race in American History," historian Barbara J. Fields isolates the post-Civil War South as a key arena for the working out of American racial definitions and dynamics. She notes that, while it did involve extending human rights and citizenship to the freedmen, the real agenda of post-war Reconstruction was only tangentially concerned with race. The goal, she says, was the same as that of other simultaneous moves toward national unity (in Japan, Germany, and Italy) that marked what would become the capitalist world. It was to establish "national unification on the basis of a system of formally free labor mediated through the market."

To accomplish this, both the former slaves and the white subsistence farmers had to be converted into wage laborers. They needed to be available to work for (small) wages in the plantation production of commodity crops (cotton, tobacco, sugar) and in the mills, mines, and factories of "the New South."

In Fields's reading, the North abandoned the freedmen when the former slaves failed to cooperate with the capitalist project. "They [the freedmen] were not dependable wage workers," she writes. In her research she found that Northern "complaints about undependable work habits echo and re-echo in the sources concerning the freedmen." Those same complaints could also be seen "...again and again, in every part of the world, whenever an employer class...has tried to induce men and women unbroken to market discipline to work in exchange for a wage. The planters, indeed, made the same complaints about the people whom they contemptuously labeled crackers [or] rednecks."

Fields emphasizes that Northern investors sincerely believed that "in offering the freedmen the chance to become free wage laborers, they were offering them a wonderful boon. But," she says, "the freedmen knew what they wanted....They wanted their own land, and the right to farm it as they chose. ...Most found bizarre the white folks' preoccupation with growing things [e.g., cotton] that no one could eat."

At the same time that "the freedmen were being hustled into the market economy," the white "yeoman farmers" were being forced into the market by debt. Both groups, Fields observes, were unhappy with this state of affairs. Both would have preferred "secure tenure of land and peace in which to pursue essentially self-sufficient farming."

At the end of the Civil War there was a call among radical Republicans for breaking up the Southern plantations and distributing the land to the freedmen. But this program was rejected by the North in favor of an alliance with the old planter class to "capitalize" and "marketize" the South. With that choice, the possibilities for a different racial equation were also diminished. Blacks and poor whites were pushed into labor market competition, instead of being placed side-by-side as neighboring, and essentially equal, subsistence farmers.

Fields believes that a post-war Southern land reform would have resulted in very different conceptions of race in contemporary America. As she puts it, a Reconstruction "program combining land distribution with debtors' relief might have permitted both freedmen and yeomen whites to live, for a time, in the essentially self-sufficient peasant manner that both groups seem to have preferred.... With a sounder material basis for political cooperation and with their grievances more in phase with each other, the yeomen and the freedmen might have been able to build a workable alliance.... Prejudice would no doubt have remained... [but]... set in a context which allowed for a less stunted and impoverished existence for both groups, and which provided a basis for political cooperation, it might have taken a less virulent and overwhelming form."

The populist uprising, fifteen years after the end of Reconstruction, offered the last chance for that kind of biracial agrarian reform. It offered the country a chance to fulfill Thomas Jefferson's vision of America as a democratic community of self-sufficient farmers. Populism, at its best, offered a chance to make that vision of America whole by extending it to the descendants of Jefferson's slaves.

## Jim Crow in the Age of Empire

None of the events in the post-Civil War South took place in a vacuum. In the rest of America, the 1870s to 1890s were also a time of enormous turmoil. That period saw the rise of the

Robber Barons and the first industrial labor unions. In some times and places the struggle between capitalists and workers was violent and revolution sometimes seemed possible. The unregulated capitalist economy went through a series of wild fluctuations including panics and depressions that led to widespread misery in the Northern farm belt. Midwestern and Western farmers were at least as motivated to rebel as were their Southern comrades.

All of this instability, of course, heightened the desire of Northern politicians and businessmen to be finished with their half-hearted attempts at reforming Southern racial practices. By the 1890s the Northern elites had cemented their natural partnership with the old Southern "Bourbon" elite. As in all colonial relationships, the partnership consisted of Northern money and management coupled to Southern cheap labor and raw materials, with profits flowing back up the metropolis.

This was the order of things which the populists promised to overturn. That is why, as noted above, in 1892 New York businessmen could quickly cough up $40,000 to defeat a single backwoods Georgia member of Congress.

The permanent solution to the populist problem presented itself in the Southern elite's proposal to disenfranchise Southern blacks. Mississippi pioneered this course of action in 1890. Other states moved toward disenfranchisement in the wake of the populist rebellion. The public rhetoric of disenfranchisement focused mostly on appeals to white supremacy and the pernicious threat of "black domination." But a class agenda was also evident in the disenfranchisement debate.

In most states, disenfranchisement was accomplished by calling a state constitutional convention. As C. Vann Woodward notes in *The Origins of the New South,* in the calls for these conventions disenfranchisement leaders always promised that no white voters would be disenfranchised by the new measures. But once in session, the conventions became instruments to, as Woodward puts it, "establish in power 'the intelligence and wealth of the South.'" This was mostly to be accomplished through property requirements, poll taxes, and literacy tests, all measures which would remove poor whites from the electorate along with the blacks.

The *New Orleans Picayune* frankly acknowledged this fact, writing that it was "just as desirous to shut out every unworthy white man as it was to exclude every unworthy Negro." A Virginia convention delegate from the Tidewater plantation region said it was "not the negro vote which works the harm [but] the depraved and incompetent men of our own race."

In his account, Woodward sums up the anti-democratic tenor of the disenfranchisement debate by noting that, "In Virginia, where the first representative assembly in the New World had met in 1619, the convention of 1901 questioned the very principle of representative government. The General Assembly was described as 'a wild rabble' which was an enemy of 'business interests' and did more harm than good."

Many lower-class whites of the time clearly saw the disenfranchisement movement as being aimed at them. Woodward quotes speeches from Virginia hill country convention delegates saying that their constituents were "very much more interested in economic questions than in questions of suffrage," and in "railroad domination than in Negro domination."

In only one state was the disenfranchising constitution put to a popular vote. That was in Alabama and there the results made it plain that there was no "white solidarity" on the question. The predominantly white upland counties of Alabama voted very heavily against the constitution while the plantation counties passed it.

The legislation authorizing the Virginia constitutional convention required that the new document be put before the people. The Alabama vote, indicating the degree of lower-class white opposition to disenfranchisement, was cast while the Virginia convention was still in session. Conscious of the threat posed by their own, even larger, poor white population, the men of the Virginia elite quite simply took the law into their own hands and forced the constitution into law without the prescribed referendum.

The debate about black disenfranchisement also connected neatly with America's move into the, equally anti-democratic, business of empire. The Supreme Court upheld the Mississippi disenfranchising laws in 1898, the year of the Spanish American War. *The Nation* magazine at the time called it "an interesting coincidence that this important decision is rendered at a time when we are considering the idea of taking in a varied assortment of inferior races in different parts of the world, which, of course, could not be allowed to vote." As Woodward aptly put it, with regard to race relations the "Mississippi Plan" became "The American Way."

As in the days of slavery, the Southern system for dealing with race was mimicked throughout the North, in diluted form. At the dawn of this century many Midwestern cities were as segregated as Southern ones. On the Eastern seaboard a black traveler had to go all the way up to New York before leaving the separate "colored" car, and even farther north before finding integrated places of eating and amusement.

This was the time when "race" as we know it was born. This is when the suppression of the African American presence became a central governing factor in American life. At the start of the American century there seemed to be an American racial consensus. This was, and would be, a white man's country. But the racial consensus would not withstand the failure of the economic order with which it was so entwined. In three decades' time it was coming unraveled again.

# CHAPTER 5

# "We Shall Not Be Moved"

*Standing Together in the Great Depression*

## Revolution in the Cotton Fields

In the spring of 1934 a secret meeting was held, under cover of darkness, in an isolated schoolhouse near the east Arkansas town of Tyronza, not far across the Mississippi River from Memphis. Twenty men were in the room that night at the Sunnyside School. The two who stood at the front, both white, were a gas station owner and a dry cleaner from town. They were both members of the Socialist Party which, in the days of Eugene Debs, before World War I, had been strong in Arkansas.

The eighteen other men were all tenant farmers. Tenant farmers in the plantation South were poor in the best of times. But in 1934 they were desperate. As part of the New Deal economic reforms most of that year's cotton crop was destroyed. In return, the federal government issued checks to compensate the farmers. But the checks went only to the landowners. Tenants received nothing. As winter closed in they were at the brink of starvation. There were no welfare benefits or food stamps back then. The tenants were living on Red Cross handouts, if anything.

In that country school room on that very night, those eighteen men became the founding members of the Southern

Tenant Farmers Union (STFU). Eleven of them were white and seven were black.

In the course of the meeting that night one of the white men stood to announce that he had previously been a member of the Ku Klux Klan. "But," he said, looking around at his black comrades, "We're all in this same predicament together now, and that's the only way we're going to get out of it—together."

The men in Sunnyside School would have remembered that fifteen years earlier many black sharecroppers on Arkansas plantations had joined an all-black group called the Progressive Farmers and Householders Union. At least twenty-five of them were killed by white mobs. An interracial organization was bound to be viewed as even more of a threat and to likewise face violent opposition. For one thing, the very meeting of a racially mixed group violated Jim Crow customs and laws.

Even more important, the profitable functioning of the plantation system depended upon the lower classes of whites identifying with their white landlords and bosses, not their black neighbors and co-workers. Segregation was intended, above all, to enforce that culture of racial solidarity. The poor whites had to be kept more interested in their whiteness than their poverty; otherwise the "leveling" threat, so feared by the Cavaliers of Old Virginia, would be unleashed again.

The official reaction to the STFU came quickly. Just a few months after the founding, C. H. Smith, a black minister and farmer, and Ward Rodgers, a white union organizer, were out in the cotton fields in Crittenden County, speaking to a group of sharecroppers, when they were arrested by the county sheriff. Rodgers, the white man, was released with the warning to stay away from the area. But Rev. Smith was imprisoned and beaten by deputy sheriffs.

The situation was a dire one for the fledgling organization. By releasing Rodgers and detaining Smith, the authorities were clearly trying to insert a racial wedge into the new union and to send a message that agitation would not be tolerated. If the STFU did not successfully resist the assault, it would be strangled in the cradle.

The first step was to get Rev. Smith a lawyer with the clout to raise his case above those of all the other jailed black men in east Arkansas. They were lucky enough to find C. T. Carpenter, a lawyer and past president of the nearby Woodland Baptist College, and a man whose father was known to have fought in the Civil War under General Robert E. Lee. Carpenter advised the union organizers that on the day Rev. Smith was brought to court they should pack the courtroom to overflowing with all of the meanest looking *white* sharecroppers and farmworkers they could find.

The union followed his advice. The judge eyed the ominous mob of poor whites before him and released the black preacher. On the strength of this successful display of interracial unity, the STFU was launched and chapters began to spring up all over east Arkansas faster than the union leaders could count them.

On September 1, 1935 the STFU decided to call for a strike during cotton picking season to demand higher wages. At the time, cotton pickers were working for as little as forty cents a day. The strike date was set for Monday, September 12. In preparation leaflets were printed and hidden at various sites around the territory. Then, at 11:00 P.M. on Sunday, September 11, union workers all over Arkansas slipped out into the night to spread the leaflets.

One of them, a black woman and a union officer, described riding up and down the streets and roadways around Gould, Arkansas, distributing strike leaflets. She was in the car "laying down on my stomach, holding the door cracked open, and I'd push the leaflets through the crack and spread them out in the street. You pick up speed and that'd just make them things go flying all over the yards." The next morning, she said, "White folks thought a plane had flown over there and spread all them leaflets. They were all over the state."

The strike was a success. Five thousand field workers stayed at home, and they won their key demand, which was for a minimum wage of a dollar a day. The strike also brought the sharecroppers' struggle to national attention. Northern newspapers covered the strike, and a Hollywood newsreel company sent a film crew to Arkansas. When the danger had passed, the newsreel company produced a film of interviews with strike participants and dramatic re-enactments of scenes from the strike, with union workers playing themselves. In movie theaters across America people saw black and poor white Southerners suffering violence and hunger together, and working side by side to secure justice.

Writing to the head of an STFU local, the union secretary and founder H. L. Mitchell cited interracial unity as the key to the STFU's success. "It is very important," Mitchell wrote, "that we organize the Whites as well as the Negroes.... There are no 'niggers' and no 'poor white trash' in the Union. These two kinds of people are all lined up with the Planters. We have only Union men in our organization, and whether they are white or black makes no difference."

The success of the strike fueled another wave of growth and the STFU quickly expanded out from Arkansas into the cotton-growing regions of Mississippi, Tennessee, southern Missouri, Texas, and Oklahoma. When delegates gathered for a convention in January 1936, the union, still less than two years old, had 35,000 members. The members were black and white together, and, in the Southwest, Mexican and Choctaw, too.

At that convention the delegates endorsed a plan, drawn up by Mitchell and a Memphis college professor, for the radical reform of American agriculture. The plan called for a national land authority to buy up all farms larger than 160 acres and redistribute the land among families or farmer cooperatives. Farmers would pay 25 percent of their crop income for rent. The authority would be governed by a board of three presidential appointees and seven members elected by farm organizations in the geographic regions of the United States.

As writer Anthony Dunbar has noted, this plan marked a unique synthesis of socialist tactics and American ideals. Land was to be expropriated and redistributed, but the goal was still the self-sufficient, self-governing, and decentralized agrarian communities of which Jefferson dreamed. This was the vision for which the STFU did battle. The union members had to be realistic about the prospects for that vision, and certainly most of their energies were devoted to immediate struggles for survival. But by joining together and building an organization they had identified themselves not just as poor and uneducated farm workers, but as actors on the stage of history. They were people worthy of a dream, and ready to change the world.

## Stranded on Highway 61

*Wholesale eviction by planters*

January 1, 1939 arrived cold and cruel in the precincts of the STFU. In 1938 the STFU had won its demand that the federal government send crop subsidy checks directly to tenants. In response, starting on New Year's Day, 1939, planters began the wholesale eviction of their tenants, and the first to go were those affiliated with the union. In the southern Missouri region along the Mississippi River, called "the boot-heel," about 2,000 evicted sharecroppers, roughly half black and half white, set up housekeeping in makeshift tents along U.S. Highway 61. They hoped to attract attention to their plight. Newspapers called it "the Missouri Highway Demonstration." But the fact was that the people on the roadside also had no other place to go.

The sharecroppers camped through most of a cold, wet winter. Their tents were made only from old blankets and they lived amidst the ruins of their belongings and their surviving farm animals. Snows came, and bitter cold rains. Some people were able to take shelter in churches and barns around the area. But hundreds were left outdoors, at the side of the road, exposed to the weather.

Pictures of the evictees appeared in the Northern newspapers, and newsreel footage again brought Southern sharecroppers into the nation's movie theaters. Eleanor Roosevelt made a public appeal for aid to the evictees. Food and proper tents were shipped in, but Missouri sheriffs kept the relief trucks from reaching the sharecroppers.

Eventually police broke up most of the highway encampments. One group of several hundred installed near New Madrid, Missouri, led by an army veteran, had trained and made plans for armed resistance. But they were tricked into giving up their weapons to board a bus ostensibly bound for a federal resettlement community. In fact, the sharecroppers were dumped in a remote swamp with no shelter, food, or tools of any kind.

In the end no authority—federal, state or local—could or would intervene to stop the evictions. The STFU never recovered from the setback.

There was a song that STFU members sang a lot. It was an adaptation of an old gospel tune that was known among Southern blacks and whites alike. You can hear the song in that newsreel footage of the 1935 cotton pickers' strike. You could hear it along the highways of southern Missouri in that desperate winter of 1939. Twenty-five years later that same song was ringing in the ears of a troubled nation, as black Southerners and their white allies sang it again along the highways and byways of the segregated South.

The song was "We Shall Not Be Moved." Those evicted tenant farmers of 1939 sang the song with ironic determination. They had already been moved, after all. But they sang it anyway, as an act of faith. That act of faith was honored twenty-five years later when black and white Americans marching together and singing that very same song forced an end to legal segregation. The song passed into history. It became part of the American story, and with it went the spirit of the STFU.

Miller Williams is a noted Southern poet. He teaches creative writing and literature at the University of Arkansas. His friend, country and western songwriter Tom T. Hall, calls Williams "the hillbilly professor." Miller Williams's daughter is Lucinda Williams, a country-rock singer-songwriter of some note, and his father was Rev. Claude Williams, one of the organizers of the STFU. Claude Williams began his life as a Presbyterian minister, but his clerical career was derailed by his passion for social justice, which put him at the center of the Southern wars for racial equality and workers' rights over three decades.

Recently Miller Williams told an interviewer that his father admitted to him that the STFU was a failure by any practical standards. But the elder Williams always insisted that the union taught the poor and working people of the mid-South two enduring and important lessons: "Number one—that they could fight for their rights, it was possible to do that. And Number two—that black and white could fight together."

## On the Right Side of History

Oliver Law was a black man born in West Texas in 1899. He grew up on a ranch and fought in World War I. After the war he re-enlisted in the army and served a total of six years. During those six years in the U.S. Army Oliver Law never rose above the rank of private first class.

After the Army, Law settled in Chicago. There he worked a number of different blue-collar jobs. He opened a restaurant for a while, but it never took off. When the Depression came in 1929, Law was just another unemployed black man on the streets of a city filled with unemployed people of all ethnic backgrounds.

But something happened during the Depression days that changed Oliver Law's life. He encountered people who seemed to understand the racism of American society and to know why there were no jobs anymore. These people also said they knew how to change things. Some of these people were white and some were black and they worked together as apparently equal partners. Of course, some of them were Communists. But unemployment and hunger made a little Bolshevism seem insignificant.

Law joined one of the Communist-led organizations for the unemployed and soon he was a leader. He organized and

spoke at rallies and was arrested several times while demonstrating against evictions. A man who met Law years later and
thousands of miles away recognized him instantly as the person he had seen at an eviction site on the South Side of
Chicago addressing the crowd from the roof of a house, before
the police pulled him down and hauled him off to jail.

The radical organizations of the Depression era were a
force for social change and a school for what the members
hoped would be a revolution. In this world Law learned about
how his history as a black man fit into the big picture of
American capitalism. He also learned about the struggles of
workers and poor people in other countries and about the
threat posed by the rise of fascism in Europe. Black radicals
on the South Side identified heavily with the struggles of
Africa. The influence of Marcus Garvey's Back to Africa movement was still strong in all the black communities of the
urban North.

When Mussolini's armies invaded Ethiopia in 1935, all the
pieces fell together for black radicals like Oliver Law. Ethiopia
was the only nation on the African continent that had never
been colonized and had never been under white rule. The fascist invasion made it clear that the interests of people of color
everywhere were inextricably linked with the anti-fascist cause.
In African American communities across the country people
raised money for aid to the Ethiopian fighters. Some black
men tried to go to Ethiopia and join the battle, but the U.S.
government prevented their departure.

Then, a few months later, in July 1936, a military uprising
led by Francisco Franco began against the democratic government of Spain. At first the government, supported by hastily
organized citizen's militias, held back the rebel officers. Then
Mussolini sent in troops to support Franco and Hitler sent
German warplanes and pilots and military advisers. The
elected government of Spain was about to be swamped by the
fascist alliance. Spanish officials pleaded for aid from France,
Britain, and the United States. But no help was forthcoming.
Only the Soviet Union came to Spain's defense.

Through the international network of Communist parties, the call quickly went out for volunteers to come and turn back the fascists in Spain. All over the world thousands of workers, students, and political activists lined up to join the International Brigades. In Chicago Oliver Law was one of several hundred Americans to answer the call. Eventually 2,800 Americans would serve in the Spanish cause. About one-third of the American volunteers were Jews who were well aware of the implications of Nazi anti-Semitism. Ninety were African Americans. The American volunteers called themselves the Abraham Lincoln Brigade.

In 1937 the United States Army was still strictly segregated. African Americans served in separate units and did the dirtiest work, under the command of white officers and with little or no opportunity for advancement. In Spain in 1937 black and white Americans served side by side in every unit. Blacks served as company commanders and political officers. A black dentist and a black nurse served in the medical unit. White Southerners, New York Jews, and South Side blacks shared a trench. In the International Brigades a person wasn't judged by race but by competence and commitment.

One of the African Americans who fought in Spain, a New Yorker named Tom Page, looked back on the experience decades later saying, "In Spain was the first time that I was truly treated like a man." Race just didn't matter to the Spanish people or to the international volunteers. The black Lincolns enjoyed the hospitality of Spanish families and courted the Spanish girls on an even par with their other comrades.

There was prejudice in the ranks. Vaughn Love, for instance, recalled a tense moment when a white American volunteer took nasty exception to "his girl" being stolen by a black man. Other African American fighters recalled scattered incidents of racial slurs or innuendo. But in every case the offense was noted and the white offender was reprimanded. There was prejudice, as there is among humans. But the coercive powers, official and otherwise, were arrayed against it, where back in America the reverse was true, and that made a difference.

Among the Americans, the most highly valued commodity wasn't white skin but military experience. The volunteers from European countries were mostly World War I veterans. But most of the Americans were in their twenties and so had been too young to serve in that war. Oliver Law, with his six years' service, which included combat experience, rose quickly through the ranks. He was a company leader in the spring of 1937 when the commander of the Lincolns was promoted to a position in the International Brigades command.

Two men with military backgrounds were available for the commander's job—Law and Walter Garland, a New Yorker. Both were African Americans. Law got the job and the Lincoln Battalion became the first racially mixed American military unit to do battle under a black commanding officer. Law served for a period of several months until he was killed in battle. In all, one-third of the American volunteers died in Spain.

Steve Nelson was the son of Croatian immigrants, a carpenter, a union organizer, and an American Communist Party activist. As political officer for the American volunteers, he was one of three people in the room when Law was selected. He later recalled that at the time he and the others were aware that they were picking a black commander and that the decision spoke well for the Lincolns' policy of interracial unity. But he did not remember that being discussed during the decision making. There was no consciousness of the historic weight that the decision would come to bear.

Also among the Americans fighting in Spain in those days was another young Texan named Robert Reed. Reed was an East Texan from a white sharecropping family. Back in East Texas he had joined the Southern Tenant Farmers Union and had become a local leader as a very young man. He was selected to attend Commonwealth College, a school in Arkansas which served to educate Southern labor and farm movement activists. He was at Commonwealth when the call for volunteers in Spain went out.

These three Americans came together in Spain with 30,000 other volunteers from virtually every nation on earth.

They came together in Spain, but they came from somewhere together, too. They came from a broad and diverse radical movement that shook the country in the Depression decade.

**Falling Apart and Pulling Together**

The Great Depression struck the American people like a runaway train. The previous half-century of industrialization and economic expansion seemed to promise a future of endless progress and prosperity. The labor uprisings and ideological turmoil of the pre-World War I period were long forgotten in the 1920s when, as President Harding put it, the business of America was business, and business had never been better.

When all of that disappeared in a flash, Americans were stunned and desperate. Prosperity, for all but the very rich, turned out to be built on sand, and the house of capital turned out to be a house of cards. Banks failed. Savings disappeared. Loans were called in. Mortgages were foreclosed. Businesses closed.

In the early years of the Depression, 25 percent of the American work force was unemployed. People who had been solidly middle class a few years before were going hungry. The really poor people were actually starving. Millions of men were hitting the road, aimlessly wandering in search of work. This went on for three full years with the U.S. government, under Herbert Hoover, doing nothing but issuing pep talks and bland assurances.

It was an apocalyptic time, and while the government fiddled, the people began to act. Many of them threw aside old ideological prejudices and considered radical solutions to the country's economic problems. Ordinary people also began to cast aside the other prejudices of race, religion, and nationality that could prevent united action. Millions of Americans—not students or bohemians or intellectuals, but ordinary workers and small merchants and middle-class professionals—set themselves to the task of making a new world. They did not do this from an excess of idealism or a psychological need to cause trouble. They did it simply from the sure sense that the old world was shot to hell and they had nothing to lose.

Alongside the growth of various radical and socialist political movements, the 1930s also saw the birth of the modern union movement with the formation of the Congress of Industrial Organizations (CIO). In the coal mines of West Virginia, the steel mills of Pittsburgh, the auto plants of Detroit, and on the docks of San Francisco, the CIO succeeded because it was able to rally workers across the old lines of ethnicity, religion, and race.

In Northern cities and factory towns that had long been a patchwork of warring ethnic enclaves, Jews, Italians, and Poles at last joined with blacks, Asians, and Hispanics to demand human dignity and a living wage. Organizations of the unemployed also served as rallying points of racial and ethnic unity in the cities during the Great Depression.

The spirit of all these working-class movements was dramatically embodied in the Abraham Lincoln Brigade. The Lincoln Brigade volunteers were mostly graduates of the labor and unemployed movements, with a few students and artists thrown in for spice. They saw their service in Spain as part of an international working-class struggle in which "an injury to one was an injury to all." Their story stands as an example of the heroic things that ordinary people can do when their sense of self, and self-interest, is joined to a clear understanding of their historical moment and a sweeping vision of the common good.

The radical vision that arose from America's cotton fields and factories in the 1930s fed into the politics of the Democratic Party and Franklin Roosevelt's New Deal coalition, and through that route it served to change the face of American society for good. Protections and benefits were guaranteed for workers and the unemployed and retirees. Public monies were appropriated on a mass scale to put people to work in projects for the public good. Business and finance were brought under public regulation to ensure the relative stability of the capitalist market.

Of course, at the end of the Depression, America went to war and that changed things even more as Americans were drawn out of their regional enclaves and thrown across the world together on a massive scale. They saved the world from German fascism and its racist horrors.

Americans of all colors came home from the war to a country that was still segregated and, on the surface at least, seeking only a return to normalcy. But beneath that surface everything had changed. The lessons the Depression and war had taught about inclusiveness and pulling together weighed heavily on the public conscience. The sacrificial contribution African Americans had made to America's reform and survival demanded respect and repayment. The wheels were turning and there would be no turning back.

# Chapter 6

# Making Room at the Table

*The Poor People's Campaign and the American Economy*

## A Rainbow Army of the Poor

Catholic Worker founder Dorothy Day often quoted a line from Dostoevsky, "Love in practice is a harsh and dreadful thing compared to love in dreams." The same could be said about an organization of the poor. It is a beautiful dream, but in practice it can be a harsh and dreadful thing. Many poor people come to an organization already traumatized by the difficult conditions of their lives. They are often deeply suspicious and distrustful, not only of the powers that be, but also of each other, and especially of anyone who claims to want to help them. An interracial coalition of the poor is perhaps the most beautiful of American dreams. In the winter of 1968, Martin Luther King, Jr. was discovering just how harsh and dreadful, and downright messy, that dream could be in practice.

In 1968 King was a global figure, a Nobel laureate, with a moral authority recognized by people of every nation and religion. By 1968 King's famous dream of August 1963 had, in large part, been written into law by the U.S. Congress. He had changed the face of America and inspired freedom fighters the world over, from South Africa to northern Ireland to Czechoslovakia. King had access to heads of state. At thirty-nine years of age, he could, if he chose, simply step back to a secure life of writing and reflection and enjoy his growing family. King was a man on top of the world and in his prime.

But rather than resting on his literal laurels, King chose to spend much of his last year in the company of garbage collectors, farm workers, coal miners, and the unemployed. Instead of accepting endless congratulations for his great dream of 1963, he was out in the streets and hollows and migrant camps, side by side with the poorest people in America, working out a new dream.

In 1968 the civil rights movement was in crisis. All of the initial demands for voting rights and desegregation had been won, at least on paper. And the unity that had coalesced around those clear and simple demands was breaking apart. The Northern white middle-class backers of the movement were moving on to Vietnam and various campus issues. Some blacks in the movement were rejecting nonviolence and integrationism in favor of black nationalism and separatism. Many were tempted by the new Black Panther Party's policy of armed self-defense.

King was working against the war, too, but he knew that was not enough. He needed to keep up the pressure on the home front. The movement had retained the allegiance and enthusiasm of its African American base because it had delivered on specific winnable demands that would directly improve the daily lives of the people. To keep up the momentum for social change, King knew that his movement had to keep delivering. He also felt a heavy responsibility to demonstrate to his own black people that nonviolence and interracial cooperation were not passive and demeaning, but could in fact be instruments of revolutionary change.

Surveying the political landscape, King concluded that, after the securing of fundamental human rights, poverty was the biggest problem facing black America. He also thought that the time was right for a militant anti-poverty crusade. Public opinion polls of the time showed a sizable majority of white Americans ready to pay more taxes in order to meet the needs of the poor. It appeared that a clear-cut demand for a guaranteed subsistence income for every American just might be winnable. And such a reform would be an important first step toward reordering the American economy around human needs instead of corporate profits.

In those days, his co-workers recall, King was talking about a fundamental redistribution of power in America. Off the record, when the tape recorders were gone, he was saying that some form of democratic socialism might be required to correct the injustices and inhumanities of American life. He expected to frame the Poor People's Campaign as a crusade for the institution of a Social and Economic Bill of Rights, guaranteeing the basic requirements of a decent life to every American.

As part of this bill of rights, every American would be guaranteed a job, if able to work, or an income sufficient to sustain a household. The campaign would begin with a trained and disciplined nonviolent army of the poor camping out in the nation's capital to press the demand for "jobs or income."

As King turned his attention to economic issues, he also saw that it was time for a new kind of interracial alliance with new kinds of allies. He looked to the poor themselves to press the demand for economic rights. The black poor alone, however, could not win such an important structural economic reform. They needed allies, so King began reaching out to Hispanics, Native Americans, and poor whites, seeking to form an interracial alliance of the poor that could shake the economic foundations of America. He needed these allies for his Poor People's Campaign to win, but King also sensed that the process of putting together an interracial coalition around common interests was an important act, in and of itself, for America's future.

Vincent Harding, historian and activist, was a close associate of King. Speaking to a black church conference in 1983 he recalled, "One of the last times I saw him was ... in Atlanta ... at a gathering that ... was one of the most exciting, stimulating and scary things I have ever seen. For the first time, Native

Americans, blacks, Hispanics, and poor whites were all beginning to talk about the ways in which we might, together, find a
way to speak to the poverty that cuts across all racial lines...."
Harding continued:

> King was trying to deal with two things there. He was
> trying to find a way of organizing folks to deal with
> poverty through some form of revolutionary nonvio-
> lence. But more important for us at this particular mo-
> ment [in 1983], this was also King's way of dealing
> with racism in American society.
>
> King said that the way you deal with racism is to
> find a common vision that will join you together. Find
> a common task on which those of all races can work
> together. That is the best way to deal with racism in
> American society. A thousand conferences will not do
> what a gathering of people can do when they are con-
> vinced that across their racial lines, they have a com-
> mon goal that they must work for, sacrifice for, and
> die for.
>
> That was the way King was moving toward dealing
> with racism. Being equal in a society like this was be-
> side the point. He was seeking to organize across racial
> lines to transform the society, not to be equal in it
> ...[to] participate in a struggle across racial lines to
> create a new non-exploitative society.

In this vision of racial justice, integration was a sharing of
power and it would come from working together on mutual
goals, not merely from legislated desegregation or from senti-
mental good feelings.

So, all that winter of 1968, between fundraising trips and
lectures, Martin Luther King, Jr. was spending his time in loud
and smoky meeting rooms, surrounded by an often discordant
rainbow of the poor. The organizing was tough. There were
plenty of old suspicions and stereotypes coming to the surface.
And the problems went in all directions. For instance, at one

point a top member of King's staff was heard to exclaim of a prominent Chicano leader, "He doesn't seem to realize that he is the child and we are the parents."

Such turf wars broke out at every turn. Many of King's associates thought that the whole idea was insane. But, even at the roughest moments, King insisted that this was the path for the movement's future. He was convinced that these meetings, where people were learning to fight, together, for their mutual interests, were laying the only viable foundations for real racial unity in America.

There was, of course, a historical foundation to King's strategy. *The Strange Career of Jim Crow* by Southern historian C. Vann Woodward was one of the "bibles" of the civil rights movement, alongside Henry David Thoreau's "On Civil Disobedience" and the Bible itself. Woodward's small volume analyzed the period after Reconstruction, when segregation was introduced, and concluded that Jim Crow was, more than anything, a response to the interracial populist "leveling" threat.

The civil rights movement of the 1960s was widely understood as a Second Reconstruction of race relations in the South. And the similarities were striking. In this Reconstruction, as in the first, Southern blacks forged an alliance with federal power and with wealthy Northern liberal patrons. This alliance forced enormous changes in the Southern landscape. And this time the changes were enduring. Southern blacks were permanently re-enfranchised. Opportunities in schooling and commerce were opened. An important blemish was removed from America's international image as the democratic leader of the Free World.

But when this had been accomplished, the interests of the federal government and the liberal elite and those of African America began to diverge. King understood this. He saw that black Americans needed to build their political future on a more durable foundation. He saw the need to reach out to lower income white people and to the other non-white minority groups, to forge coalitions of mutual self-interest.

In short, Martin Luther King, Jr. saw that the coming of the Second Reconstruction opened the way for a revival of the populist dream. If King had lived, this enduring dream could very well have changed America almost beyond recognition. It still could.

## Lost Moments and Shrinking Pies

In all of its most important aspects, the Poor People's Campaign planned by Martin Luther King was solidly in the American tradition of social movements that cross racial lines in the service of a common good. In discussing his plans, King recognized this historic linkage and he saw himself picking up the fallen mantle of the 1890s and 1930s. The Depression-era hunger marches in Washington, DC were cited as the explicit model for the Southern Christian Leadership Conference's Resurrection City.

King invited the poor to reach beyond their pain and suspicion and move toward their genuine interests. He invited them to become the bearers of new values for America, the witnesses who would turn the conscience of the nation away from materialism, racism, and war and toward a new America of cooperation and equality.

But in some other important ways, King's Poor People's Campaign was very much a creature of its own, late 1960s, historical moment. And a short moment it turned out to be. The vision and world view of the Poor People's Campaign, and of all 1960s social movements, was grounded in the reality of unprecedented, and seemingly boundless, American prosperity.

America emerged from World War II with the only fully functioning industrial economy on the planet. All of the European and Asian competition had been crippled by the bombs and shells of combat while our factories, highways, and railroads sat secure behind the great moat of two oceans. But that brought no guarantee of postwar prosperity. America's problem was that our productive capacity far exceeded the demand of the world market. In addition, there were millions of soldiers and sailors coming home to seek civilian jobs.

The war lifted America out of the Great Depression. But there was a very real prospect that once the war was over depression would return. And indeed the first postwar years were marked by economic recession. To head off another depression, and the popular upheaval it would bring, the Truman administration set out on a massive program of economic stimulus and planning. The postwar economic program seamlessly interwove foreign and domestic policy under the single overarching concern of "national security."

On the home front, the G.I. Bill sent millions of war veterans to college and set them up with easy credit for home purchases. Under the cover of preparing for national defense, a network of interstate, multi-lane, limited-access superhighways was built. This allowed millions of Americans to move out of the cities and buoyed the demand for automobiles.

In foreign affairs, the Marshall Plan shored up capitalism on the continent and secured Western Europe as a ready market for American-made goods. Meanwhile, the Cold War policy of "global containment" of the Soviet threat kept defense budgets at wartime levels, even before Korea. In Cold War America, national defense no longer meant defending our shores, it meant putting troops in the field wherever Western economic and political dominance was resisted, anywhere on earth.

All of these policies combined to keep America's wartime economic expansion going all the way through the 1950s and 1960s. Household incomes grew sharply and steadily. Almost an entire generation of white people entered the middle class for the first time. Their children grew up thinking of college education and home ownership as divine birthrights. Just one rung down the ladder, America's blue-collar industrial workers were the kings of the proletarian planet. They owned homes with lawns and central heat and air conditioning. Some of them even had two automobiles.

Affluent new suburbs sprang up at every exit on those federally funded superhighways. Every day in every way, life for the majority of Americans was getting better and better, and they had no reason to think that the good times would ever end. This was no Roaring Twenties bubble waiting to burst; this was a new kind of American prosperity, underwritten and insured by the U.S. government. It was as stable as the Washington Monument and secured by the U.S. Marines.

America's big thinkers and official intellectuals called what was happening "the end of ideology." They said that all of America's structural issues had been resolved. We were a classless society with no substantial fissures or zones of dissonance. The only political questions remaining were ones of management and technique. And anyone who disagreed could tell it to Senator Joe McCarthy.

American postwar prosperity continued on through the 1960s, but the great social silence associated with "the end of ideology" was shattered at the dawn of that decade. The clarions of the American eschaton had neglected to note one glaring piece of unfinished business. With very few exceptions, black Americans were shut out of the new affluence. In one-third of the states in the union they were legally segregated from whites in most public places. In most of the old Confederacy they were denied the right to vote. They received woefully substandard education and were largely without opportunity for advancement.

In fact, for much of black America in the boom years of the 1950s, things were actually getting worse. The mechanization of Southern agriculture meant the end of most farm labor and a drastic scaling back of the sharecrop system. Most Southern blacks were, as the British say, "redundant." Many fled North in search of factory jobs. For those who remained, misery deepened.

Black Americans had lost their small toehold on the land in the South. But the Cold War brought them a major claim on America's ideological capital. When it was introduced at the turn of the century, black disenfranchisement was seen as consistent with America's emerging role as the "protector" of various darker peoples. But in postwar imperialism, the ethos of "the white man's burden" was replaced by the banner of "The Free World." And now it was an embarrassment for ten percent of our citizenry to be disenfranchised and segregated. Embarrassment about America's "race problem" was especially acute when dealing with troublesome postcolonial leaders in Africa and Asia.

In the 1950s black Americans lived amidst a culture of rising expectations but saw their own status diminished. In the South they began to step out in protest. The Montgomery bus boycott was first, in 1955–1956. Then the student sit-ins began in 1960 and an unstoppable avalanche of black protest was rolling.

In effect, black Americans stepped out and announced that the postwar American emperor had no clothes. Once that news was out, everything else about the society came under question. The picture was completed by Michael Harrington's influential book *The Other America*. Harrington's work aimed to point out the "pockets of poverty" that persisted in affluent America. He found poverty to be widespread among the elderly, in some isolated rural populations, and among the racial minorities.

The civil rights movement and *The Other America* framed the discourse of dissent for the 1960s. Protest was raised on behalf of those who had been left out of the affluence and freedom enjoyed in the American mainstream. The bounty of the American economy was seen to be so great that the excluded minorities could be brought into the mainstream without any significant cost to anyone. The appeal was to the conscience of white, middle-class America to make a little more room at the table.

In practice, the dissident discourse of the 1960s assumed that there was no commonality of interest between the middle class and the poor, other than a moral or spiritual one. In material terms the middle-class American majority was in a position of "giving" and the poor were in the position of "receiving." In effect, the claims of the poor were being laid against the prosperity of the average American. The disjuncture may have been muted by a moral vocabulary of protest, but this approach still contained the seeds of an "us vs. them" opposition between the poor and the middle class.

At the beginning of the 1960s the claims on behalf of the poor were made through spiritual witness and self-sacrifice. As the decade of protest wore on, the claims made for "the poor" grew more strident and punitive. This was especially so among the children of the white middle class who tended to lay at the feet of their parents all the woes of the underdeveloped and malnourished Third World.

**Are the Good Times Really Over for Good?**

This was all well and good, at least in political terms, for so long as the middle class continued to benefit from the American economy. But that state of affairs turned out to be less permanent than anyone had dreamed. The great postwar economic expansion ended in 1973. It took a while for all the effects to become visible, but the fact remains that just five years after the tumult of 1968 the very foundations of American society had changed. Economic growth rates began to slow. Incomes began to stagnate. Permanent unemployment rates climbed. On the whole, the standard of living stopped getting better for most Americans.

Looking back over twenty years of long-term trends, we can see that many of those changes were inevitable. The economies of Western Europe and Japan recovered. They stopped being passive clients and became competitors. First they were manufacturing their own products for their own markets. Before long, we were buying their goods, too. And not just transistor radios and shoes, either, but basic industrial products like steel and machine tools and automobiles.

Given the American elite's ideological commitment to free trade, the movement of economic power toward Japan and Western Europe was as predictable as the movement of the tides. But the change in America's economic status came to a head in 1973 when that long-term trend combined with two immediate crises. One was the OPEC oil boycott. In retaliation for U.S. aid to Israel during the October War, the petroleum-exporting countries of the Middle East banded together and refused to sell oil to the United States.

For the first time since the Great Depression, Americans tasted the terror of scarcity. There were long lines and rationing for gasoline and fuel oil. Thermostats were set chillingly low. Speed limits were lowered. City lights were dimmed, even at Christmas. In a flash the foundations of our prosperity were exposed, and they were not invulnerable.

The other thing that happened beginning in 1973 was that the toll the Vietnam War was taking on the American economy became visible. For ten years, when we should have been updating and reforming our economy to meet the challenge of new competition, we were instead sending the best of our human and material resources down a sinkhole in Southeast Asia. In 1965 Lyndon Johnson made a strategic decision that he would try and fight the war off the books, without raising taxes and without cutting domestic spending. As the war dragged on, this deception wore thin. Its effects weakened the American economy and undermined American credibility in the world market.

The flaws in the American economy became apparent in 1974 when the country went into what was at the time its deepest economic downturn since the Great Depression and stayed in it for a year and a half. When the economy bounced back it never got back up to pre-1973 growth levels. Around this time country singer Merle Haggard wrote and recorded one of his "voice-of-the-people" songs about America. He called this one, "Are the Good Times Really Over for Good?"

From the mid-1970s onward the story is familiar. In the late 1970s Americans started buying energy-efficient Japanese cars. Massive layoffs hit the auto industry and the Steel Belt turned to rust. In the early 1980s American agriculture went into a depression that all but wiped out the family farm. In every area of the economy, U.S. corporations shipped the high-paying blue-collar jobs overseas. For those still working, wages stopped going up.

In 1996 it usually takes two incomes to maintain a middle-class standard of living in America. Of course that leaves too little time for a healthy family life, and sometimes even two jobs aren't enough. The recession that began in 1991, the one that gave us "downsizing," bit even deeper into the upper reaches of the middle class. In brief, the American middle-class standard of living and quality of life have steadily and drastically degenerated for two full decades.

For the poor what has been lost in the age of decline is not just income but hope. The blue-collar jobs that have disappeared from the American economy are the very ones that historically were the first rung on the ladder up from poverty. Only the crack trade has emerged to replace them, and that is the ultimate short-term solution.

During the decades of decline the wealthiest Americans have, as always, fixed the rules to protect themselves. They have done very well. For instance, in the first term of the Reagan presidency the richest 20 percent of the population gained $25 billion in annual income while the poorest 20 percent lost $6 billion. This was mostly the result of spending cuts on programs for the poor and tax cuts for the rich. When the dust had cleared from the Reagan revolution, that top 20 percent was taking in 43 percent of all family income in America, while the bottom 20 percent was scraping by on 4.7 percent.

At the same time everyone else—poor, working poor and middle class alike—has suffered. For instance, one study of laid-off steelworkers in Chicago found that when they went back to work their incomes declined from an average of $22,000 a year to $12,500. Those workers were once middle class and are now working-poor. Of course they have suffered to varying degrees. But the differences between the poor and the middle class are now matters of degree, and that is an important change in the American scene.

In 1968 it seemed that America's social injustices could be cured by a new apportionment of an ever-expanding pie. Five years later the pie was shrinking and the questions were much tougher. Everything had changed except the thinking of most

American liberals and radicals. They kept living in 1968 and went on decrying the materialism and selfishness of that great enemy of humanity, the American white middle class. Meanwhile, that same white middle class, in close touch with the tax form and the mortgage payment, got the creeping sense that the American Dream machine wasn't working for them anymore, either.

In the 1960s the most important and unrecognized fact about American society was the persistence of poverty in the midst of prosperity. In the 1990s the most important, and mostly unrecognized, fact is the very real potential for an alliance of self-interest between the poor and the middle class, regardless of race.

For the most part the upheavals that struck America in the 1960s were one-time-only events. They were the product of a place in time where demographic and economic trendlines converged. The baby boom met the postwar economic boom and an explosion happened. The explosion was social, political, and cultural. The political manifestations proved ephemeral. But much of the cultural explosion endured.

A great deal of the cultural legacy from that odd time has proven irrelevant, or downright destructive, such as the single-minded emphasis on self-fulfillment. Some of it has not. For better and worse, American culture in the 1990s is not what it was forty years ago, and how people think about race has been one of the main areas of cultural change.

CHAPTER 7

# American Roots Rainbow

*The Social Vision of Popular Culture*

Every spring thousands of people travel to a racetrack in New Orleans to hear America sing. The songs they hear are about Jesus and Stagger Lee and Casey Jones. The songs call up fire from the bayous of the Choctaw and the Houma and the long-dead Tchoupitoulas. They sing about working on the railroad and cutting the cane. The songs and the singers come in all colors and the colors merge in the racetrack mud of sweat and beer. The drumbeat of West Africa runs like a steady, life-giving pulse through them all.

One hundred and fifty years ago Walt Whitman heard America singing, too. He even went to New Orleans once, but he couldn't take the heat. Now much of New Orleans is air-conditioned and people go there from all over the world. They go especially to that racetrack during the last weekend of April and the first weekend of May for the New Orleans Jazz and Heritage Festival. There, under blazing sun or torrents of rain, they sometimes find their true country and they hear it sing.

Way back in the early 1970s the Jazz and Heritage Festival was organized by an assortment of Southern-fried radicals and hippies. Those founders had an idea that the interracial cultural heritage of New Orleans and South Louisiana might become an invaluable resource for building the new post-segregation

South. Today that humble event has grown into a two-weeks-a-year cultural monument that is also, not coincidentally, a mainstay of the New Orleans tourism industry.

When you go to the Jazz and Heritage Festival you encounter a tent city of American cultures. Scattered around the vast racetrack infield are tent-covered music stages devoted to the sounds of blues, jazz (old-style and new), rhythm and blues, zydeco, Cajun, country, Caribbean and African, and, most especially, gospel. Other tents are given over to storytelling and dancing and traditional crafts. Looming over one end of the racetrack is a huge arched gate bearing a message that beckons visitors to find their roots in Africa, home of the world's oldest human culture.

And Africa is the common ancestor of all the American cultural forms spread across the racetrack city. The white Cajun and country music is descended from the Celts, but the American version is very different, and the differences come from the miscegenation that defines Southern and American culture. To put it most simply, rural American music swings with a rhythm that was unknown to Old World Bretons and Scots.

Historically all of the cultural traditions of the New World have converged in New Orleans after arriving from points up the big river, down the Gulf, and across the Caribbean. This convergence has included the cultures of Spain, France, West Africa, England, Italy, Ireland, and the Jewish diaspora, all laid over the base of the Native Indian presence. In the countryside west of the city a more specific rural heritage is found among descendants of the Acadian (now "Cajun") refugees and the French-speaking blacks who have lived and worked alongside the Cajuns in slavery and in freedom.

The cultural tradition that has emerged from the cauldron of South Louisiana is no longer the property of any one of the constituent ethnic groups. It is a Creole tradition. Over the centuries "Creole" has become a very murky term, especially in South Louisiana. Today, in popular usage, it most often refers to people of mixed African and French ancestry. But originally

Creole was the name for any person born in the New World. It referred specifically to the melding of Native Indian, African, Spanish, and French cultures and bloodlines that was occurring in the early Caribbean colonies. This process was sometimes called "Creolization" and it resulted in a new thing, the Creole, that was more than the sum of its parts and was seen as the new indigenous culture of the New World.

Creolization is not all that different from the old American notion of the melting pot. The problem with the American melting pot was always the coercive element. Rather than a give and take among cultures, it often meant that other peoples were simply melted down and reshaped into imitation Anglo-Saxons, like it or not. But in the Caribbean and South America the process of cultural exchange sometimes worked more freely. This was in no small part due to the dominance of Catholicism with its impulse for the universal and its drive to synthesize. The Protestant sects of North America were the descendants of European nation-state churches and so provided little common ground for trans-ethnic exchange.

So the tradition of the Creole entered North American culture via the acquisition of New Orleans, a very old French Catholic, and almost Caribbean, city. And from that seed has grown much that is vital and hopeful in American popular culture. In the end what the visitor encounters every spring at the New Orleans racetrack is America summarized and intensified. This cultural heritage, as it has spread across the nation and into the world, has become the beating heart of America's popular culture. It represents the best of our struggle to become one nation, distilled to sound and motion, under a groove.

America's popular music traditions grow from the American South. They are Africa plus whatever else came down the river. New Orleans is the point where all the waters join and the spirit drinks most deeply. From these roots has grown a set of interracial American cultural traditions that, as the Jazzfest founders suspected, could serve as a point of unity and convergence spilling over into the rest of life.

## Good Times and the Common Good

On an autumn night toward the end of 1988, my wife and I were at John F. Kennedy Stadium in Philadelphia, Pennsylvania. We were there for the only East Coast performance of the Amnesty International Human Rights Now tour featuring Tracy Chapman, Yousef N'Dour, Peter Gabriel, Sting, and Bruce Springsteen.

The message of the Amnesty International world tour was centered on the United Nation's Universal Declaration of Human Rights. As the tour made its way from Eastern to Western Europe and from North to South America and on to southern Africa, it left in its wake hundreds of thousands of copies of the declaration printed in the local languages with the admonition to "know your rights and use them." The Universal Declaration, by the way, includes social and economic rights, some of which don't always accrue to free persons when they're born in the U.S.A.

It was a long trip to Philadelphia that night. And if the truth be told, we didn't make it solely for Amnesty International and human rights. We also made it for the idea that rock and roll, which made our own lives a better place, can, in some small way, do the same for the world—and, of course, to see the one with whom that idea is largely synonymous, "The Boss."

Bruce Springsteen's participation in the Amnesty tour was of a piece with the direction his career took starting in 1984–1985. Springsteen is the son of a New Jersey factory worker who, when laid off at the plant, sometimes worked as a bus driver and a prison guard. Bruce Springsteen comes from America's blue-collar working class. That has always been the core of his audience. Those are the people he has always sung for and about. In the late 1970s and early 1980s those people, Springsteen's people, experienced an economic disaster as America's manufacturing economy shut down and blue-collar wages started to shrink.

On his "Born in the U.S.A." tour, in the year of the Reagan re-election, Springsteen began linking the populist sympathies long present in his music with the concrete needs and aspirations of his audience and their devastated communities. At each tour stop, The Boss visited with representatives of a local community organization—a union food bank here, an environmental group there, a Saul Alinsky-style organizing project down the road. He gave the organizers a five-figure check and invited them to set up tables at his show. He also incorporated a short talk of his own about the group and its issues into the performance each night.

What was most important about that tour was not the money that was spread around, although that was good, too. The greater significance lay in the style and language Springsteen developed for explaining his activities and communicating his message. As a creative artist, he couched his politics in a cliché-free idiom which defied conventional ideologies and orthodoxies. He didn't shy away from controversy. This was not lowest-common-denominator charity. The union groups and others Springsteen associated with were grassroots renegades, often radicals. And Springsteen never missed a chance to place the blame for homelessness and unemployment at the door of Ronald Reagan's Oval Office and the corporate constituency Reagan served.

But Springsteen also didn't speak the language of protest, or even of politics in the debased sense that term now carries. He offered instead a street-level translation of that grand old construct, The Common Good. In Springsteen's declaration of interdependence it came out, "Nobody wins unless everybody wins." He spoke of rights saying, "When I was a kid, rock and roll was saying one thing, 'Let Freedom Ring!'," and of responsibilities, taking a breath and adding, "But remember, you gotta fight for it."

All of that and more was present in Springsteen's performance on the Amnesty tour. That night, aside from being moved, physically and emotionally, by the music, I was struck again with the power of Springsteen's message-stories. His spoken narratives were like the music. Both faced up to the meanest of life's realities and, as another rocker once said, "dance all over them." Both music and message were relentlessly affirmative and straight from the heart, with a minimum of decorative trappings or self-involvement.

What Springsteen did, at his best, was use the most fundamental human and humane values (interdependence and the common good) to frame his "issues" in positive terms that invite a positive response. This is in place of doom-mongering and nay-saying, which invite only despair, or a cult of political correctness, which invites only self-marginalization. Springsteen's political message and medium didn't invite alienation. They offered the rewards of community, the intrinsic good, good feelings, and good times that are found in giving oneself to something larger than oneself.

That night in Philly Springsteen sang and spoke about America's abandoned industrial communities and her homeless. He talked about social rights to work and a home and respect and a decent life. He also sang "Good Golly, Miss Molly" and somersaulted across the stage. By the spirit and sound and sense of his performance and his communication with the crowd, Springsteen suggested, in the most compelling of terms, that the freedom-in-unity (and vice versa) of a well-spent Saturday night could also be carried over to the real world of Monday morning.

At the end of the long evening, all of the musicians came back onto the stage. They all linked arms—black, white and brown—and sang the Amnesty tour's theme song, "Get up, stand up, stand up for your rights." The song comes from Bob Marley, the Jamaican reggae artist who died of cancer in 1981. Marley was a mystic man, a follower of the Rastafarian religion and a prophet of Third World revolution. Perhaps the high point of his career came when he headlined at the inaugural celebration of Robert Mugabe, the first elected leader of free Zimbabwe.

Bob Marley, the Pan-African freedom fighter, was also a devotee of American rhythm and blues music who, for a time before his career took off, lived in Wilmington, Delaware, just a short hop across the river from JFK Stadium.

He had a factory job there. He drove a forklift on the night shift. In the story of American popular culture, everything runs together.

The Amnesty International tour played Harare, Zimbabwe, too. They played in the same stadium where Marley had celebrated the victory over British colonialism. There Bruce Springsteen also found fans. They were young white South Africans who knew his work from his records and had driven long hours across the border to see him because Springsteen, like every self-respecting rocker of the time, boycotted the land of apartheid. Some of Springsteen's fans who made the trek to Harare were South African draft resisters. They had been to prison for their refusal to fight in apartheid's army, and would probably go to prison again. In his performance that night, Springsteen talked about the draft resisters. He reminded all of his fans in white South Africa that they had to fight for freedom, too, until everybody won.

**Roots for a Change**

It is fashionable today to be cynical about politicians, and, as president, Bill Clinton has given us things to be cynical about. From the vantage point of 1996, it is easy to forget the remarkable confluence of popular anger and hope that accompanied his rise to the White House. In 1992 Bill Clinton became the first presidential politician to effectively tap American middle-class fears about the shrinking economy and to make them the foundation of a winning multiracial political alliance. He was also the first of his kind to tap the progressive and unifying possibilities of American popular culture as a medium for his message.

The climactic event of the 1992 Clinton campaign was also the first, and perhaps still the most successful, event of the Clinton presidency. That was the January 1993 inaugural. In that series of public events the new president and his campaign strategists attempted to encapsulate dramatically the foundational themes of Clinton's political success.

Central to those themes were the interdependence of America's ethnic and cultural communities. In the events of the inaugural the Clinton camp sought to express an overarching, national sense of community that was rooted in common values and a common destiny. Underlying this was a generational appeal chiefly rooted in the widely shared perception that America faces an economic crisis of historic proportions.

The Clinton team has so far failed miserably at translating those ideas and impulses into public policy. But we should remember that, as public political theater on a grand scale, the events of the Clinton inaugural did work. People responded to them. There was, for a few weeks, a palpable sense of hope in the country at large. It turned up in the opinion polls and on the streets. The events worked because they tapped into the moral energy that is available to change and renew America.

The inaugural events began, as the fall Clinton-Gore campaign had begun, with a bus trip. The bus tours were a powerful motif throughout the 1992 campaign. They summoned a rich variety of associations. They were populist—the bus is the most proletarian type of transportation. They sounded the old chords of civil rights-era idealism with resonances of the Freedom Rides, and even the Montgomery bus boycott.

Perhaps most notably, the bus tours carried associations with popular culture. Country and western and rhythm and blues musicians and gospel singing groups tour America on buses like the one Clinton took. These folk artists of the electronic age are famous for sailing the highways in shiny, customized old Greyhounds from which they emerge nightly to commune with the masses from whom they draw their artistic power. That was the subtextual model and image of the Clinton-Gore bus trips.

The Last Big Cruise of the Clinton campaign began outside Charlottesville, Virginia at Monticello, the historic home of Thomas Jefferson, the ambivalent founder of American populism and ideologist of democracy. From there the bus rolled north to the Capital City, with a midpoint stop for worship at a Southern Baptist Church.

This raised the bus tour image to mythic proportions. Once again, the pictures from Monticello said, a unifying voice of freedom and equality was coming, from the South, to steer the nation back to the entirely imaginary purity of its mostly imagined roots.

When the Clinton entourage arrived in Washington, it wasn't greeted by diplomatic pomp or military display. It was greeted instead by a multiethnic festival of American popular culture. The people who put on the New Orleans Jazz and Heritage Festival were enlisted to fill the vast public space of the Washington Mall with a monument to the energy and egalitarian soul of American-roots culture. There were blues singers and gospel choirs and bluegrass fiddlers and conjunto accordions, and rock and roll bands, too. It was called An American Homecoming and it ran for a week before the inauguration.

Maya Angelou's poetry reading at the actual Inaugural Ceremony should be seen as the capstone of this cultural celebration. Angelou is an Arkansan, like the president, but she is also a black woman whose art comes from a life steeped in oppression and sorrow. She was chosen for the inaugural slot because she embodies the power of American mass culture, which is, at its white-hot core, a culture of aspiring outsiders struggling to forge a community from their aspirations.

That culture has absorbed the contributions of all comers to these shores—immigrant, exile and captive alike—and has sometimes served to bring us together when everything else conspired to drive us apart. Much is said today, especially in election years, about the debilitating influence of American pop culture. It is a commercial carrier of violence, misogyny, and blind avarice. That is all true. But it is not the whole truth. Here at home and around the world, American pop culture is often also a rainbow sign of liberation and equality.

That is because American pop culture is mostly the democratic product of America's outsiders. American movies and music, which are the heart of the nation's soul, are almost exclusively the work of blacks, Jews, gays, and the white-Southern and urban-ethnic working class.

For at least the past forty years, the dominant force in American popular culture has been rock and roll music in its various forms, all of which are simply mutations of rhythm and blues. In those decades, through the medium of the music, the African American story passed into the mainstream American mythos, via the post-Elvis generations.

Many white members of that, and subsequent generations, adopted the black story as *the* American story, mediated through the blues and the civil rights movement. They adopted it as a guiding narrative, of sorts. It was a process of appropriation similar to that of the enslaved Africans upon these shores, who adopted the Jewish story of the Exodus to their own ends. For the baby boom and later generations, the story of rock and roll, and the parallel story of the civil rights movement, are the cultural touchstones that frontier tales and World War II were to earlier generations.

Bill Clinton is an American of that generation and a former rhythm and blues musician at that. It is no accident that the first American president to have a little bit of Elvis in him is also the political operator who has most successfully played the changes of our turn-of-the-century culture. As such, Clinton is the creature of a historical transition. His successes and his failures alike serve to demonstrate where the possibilities for hope and change might lie in the new environment of a post-civil rights, post-rock and roll America.

As the Reagan presidency proved with its Star Wars flash and Rambo fear-mongering, pop cultural imagery is not a trivial thing. The world of pop culture is the world in which the American people live. That world can indeed be violent and greedy and misogynist, but it can also be democratic and tolerant and communitarian. Both sets of impulses are there. They are real. They are at least as American as violence and cherry pie, and they are the common inheritance of everyone born in, or admitted to, the U.S.A., regardless of color.

## A Culture in Common

We hear a lot today about how divided we Americans are in culture. That is true. We are divided, but the divisions are not necessarily ones of race. For instance, as this book was written, a series of stories appeared on newspaper front pages noting the chasm between black and white TV viewing habits. For instance, *Seinfeld*, on NBC, is the most popular situation comedy among white viewers. It has virtually no black audience. In black America, Fox's *Living Single* is the most popular show of any genre but it ranks low on overall viewer ratings because of its small white viewership.

This was a significant story for what it told us about the increasing fragmentation of the television audience. But there is an equally telling story in the rise of the Fox Network itself. The meteoric rise of the fourth network was made possible by the consolidation of the black audience with the youth market and the neglected blue-collar white viewers. It also helped that the network's programmers had a flair for the rude and flamboyant, and the steady underpinning of media emperor Rupert Murdoch's billions.

In part, the rise of Fox tells a neglected story of race and class in American culture, one that is written in the demographic breakdown of television ratings. The Fox Network entered the field to take advantage of the cable-era fragmentation in the TV audience. In the mid-1980s cable service became all but universal among the upper-middle-class viewers most sought by corporate advertisers. As a result, programming on the traditional broadcast networks turned toward luring upper-income viewers away from cable. They did this by offering an endless stream of shows about the travails and hijinks of well-to-do lawyers, doctors, and ad men (*L.A. Law, St. Elsewhere, Thirtysomething*, etc.).

This left a huge working-class, and still largely uncabled, audience out in the cold. Fox rushed into the vacuum. Most of Fox's programming is mediocre. The network's first flagship hit, *Married With Children*, is downright squalid. Its next one,

*The Simpsons* may be the best program in the history of the medium.

But quality is not the point here. The point is that, at least in the case of all those *Living Single* vs. *Seinfeld* newspaper stories, knee-jerk attention to race can blind us to the more creative possibilities that can arise from our popular culture as it is both shaped and consumed by its audiences.

Rap music is often cited as one of the symptoms of cultural division and decline. Rarely do the anti-rap diatribes pause to note the fact that the rap music audience is much more racially integrated than the rock or soul audiences of the 1960s ever were. In fact, the most controversial "hardcore" rappers are the ones with the largest white audiences, a fact of at best ambiguous import, since it may mean that the popularity of the "hardcore" stars stems in part from their seeming confirmation of white racist stereotypes about black brutality.

In all the verbiage directed at rapper Ice T's song, "Cop Killer," it was rarely reported that the song came from an album in which Ice T fused rap and heavy metal rock styles in an overt attempt to build a class-based rock and rap coalition. But whether the arbiters of mainstream culture can see it or not, that coalition does exist at the record stores and in the concert halls. Its members took to their respective streets during the Los Angeles riots of 1992 when white youths trashed the Westwood district while blacks burned South Central and Hispanics raged in East L.A. This coalition of the disaffected is still out there if the means and opportunity for a constructive social expression should arise.

During a break in the writing of this book, at a country music performance in West Virginia, I happened to see a white working-class boy, about twelve years old, who had obviously been brought to the event by his parents. The boy was wearing the now-familiar hip-hop uniform of baggy shorts, high top sneakers, and an oversized T-shirt. His shirt bore a promotion for the movie *Panther*, an unabashed celebration of the Black Panther Party's early days written and directed by black artists. Whatever mixed signals that picture may evoke, it is certainly not a picture of an America irredeemably divided by cultural misunderstanding.

In fact, when we talk about our divisions today we forget how truly divided we were just three decades ago. Until the 1960s, most white Americans encountered black people only as musicians or athletes or comedians. For most whites, Amos and Andy, Jackie Robinson, Pearl Bailey, and Joe Louis were black America. Perhaps you could add Duke Ellington and Billie Holiday for the sophisticated fringe, but black religion, politics, visual art, literary culture, family life, and so on, were off the map of mainstream America.

In those days, of course, black people knew a lot more about white people, but most blacks knew whites only as figures of power or menace. They saw white lives. White TV and movies comprised their daily diet, too. But they saw them at a distance, from the balcony of the movie theater, or in completely segregated settings. They did not see the white people watching themselves and reacting to themselves, and so, despite all the exposure, blacks often knew little about white people's real lives.

Today we are much more mixed up, and it is good. It's not always easy or comfortable, but it is good. We seem more divided because race relations are often tense, but that is because we live much of our lives at much greater proximity. There is tension, but now the tension can be creative as well as destructive.

The creative American possibilities of the new American culture can be glimpsed in moments of epiphany and communion. They can even be worked into a pageant of democracy, such as the Clinton inaugural. But as the subsequent years of the Clinton administration have demonstrated, no one anywhere on the conventional political scene has figured out how to turn the best possibilities of America's rainbow culture into a working, multiracial, democratic civil community.

Our popular culture is the common language of the American people. It is the means of communication. But it can't tell us *what* to say. For that we need roots that go even deeper than

America's African and immigrant cultural traditions. We need roots that go back to our very sources as human beings. For almost all Americans, those kinds of roots are planted in the faith and morality of the Judeo-Christian religious tradition, and that is where many Americans today are most effectively putting together the pieces of their communities and creating a new vision for their country.

# CHAPTER 8

# "Because He Made So Many of Them"

*The Democratic Hope of Church-Based Community Organizations*

### Reweaving the Fabric

At least twice in the past decade or so I have sat in rooms where I saw the future of American public life. Both times I joined gatherings of ordinary Americans where race didn't seem to matter much. In both cases the groups were almost equally black, white, and Hispanic in make-up. But there was not much talk about diversity, and there were no workshops on multiculturalism. The people in those rooms were diverse, in both income and ethnicity, but they were much more interested in the things that united them as representatives of their families, communities, and faith traditions.

There was no suppression of ethnic heritage in those rooms, at least none that I could see, and I was looking for it. When prayers were said, the black Baptists responded audibly, as they would in their own churches. Hispanics spoke Spanish to one another and English, or both, to the group at large. But amidst those obvious differences, there was a pervasive and uplifting understanding that among these people race and ethnicity were not walls, or weapons. They were, instead, gifts to be shared for the sake of a common good.

Both of these gatherings were meetings of people active in church-based community organizations. They were people who had come together, on the basis of shared Judeo-Christian values, to further their common interest in improving the life of their communities.

In a seafood restaurant off a back road in the pine-barren swamps of southeastern Louisiana, I dined with forty or so community leaders from Alabama, California, Colorado, Louisiana, and New Jersey. It was just after the New Year's holiday and the group in the restaurant had just completed a week of training to become more effective organizers in their congregations and neighborhoods.

The training they experienced was run by the Pacific Institute for Community Organization (PICO). It did not focus on lobbying or demonstrating or election campaigns, or any of the other things commonly considered the tools of political action. Instead, the trainers and the community leaders worked together to bring to the surface and identify, first, their own most deeply held values and, second, their concerns about the life of their community.

The most important skill the community leaders learned was to listen, really listen, to their neighbors and parishioners, to hear the things that they held most dearly in common. They were taught to build relationships, one by one, and ultimately to reweave the fabric of their communities so that it served the interests of ordinary families.

Reweaving the fabric of community, they learned, also meant learning to claim and maximize their power as citizens and children of God. To understand the function of power in a community of relationships, these grassroots leaders, many with only high school educations, read a long section from Thucydides' "History of the Peloponnesian Wars." Then they spent part of their week role-playing a negotiation between the beleaguered Melians and the mighty Athenians. Each leader also spent considerable time and effort committing to paper an explanation of the five things that were most important in their lives.

At the closing dinner, when I joined them, the group freely laughed and sang songs. By the time I arrived, the geographic and ethnic groupings had broken down. The banquet room looked like a utopian advertisement for Brotherhood Week. But race, as such, had been only at the margins of the agenda all week. Instead, discussion had turned to common concerns such as vacant housing, youth unemployment, and conditions in the public schools, and how the power of the people could bring about solutions to those problems.

The big event of this concluding banquet was an interminable in-house skit satirizing, in excruciating detail, the performance of one of the trainers. It could have been a group of kids at the end of summer camp except for the understood assumption that all the laughter went alongside some serious business. The next day these people would all go back to their families and churches and neighborhoods and try to communicate a new optimism about what was possible for ordinary people like themselves.

The other room where I saw the future was a big one. It was the gymnasium of a Catholic high school in Houston, Texas. There on a hot night at the end of July, 1,500 leaders of congregation-based organizations gathered for a voter registration and education rally. Like the city they represented, the community leaders were almost equally divided among whites, blacks, and Mexican Americans.

Through their churches these people had become part of an alliance, called The Metropolitan Organization (TMO), which extended through the whole Houston metropolitan area. That alliance was in turn linked with seven similar organizations throughout Texas organized by the Industrial Areas Foundation (IAF), the institution founded by community organizing legend Saul Alinsky.

When I visited Houston in 1985, this Texas network was changing the political landscape of the state. This was evident from the fact that the lieutenant governor, Ray Hobbie, was at the Houston meeting I attended. He was there to speak to the group and to answer their questions about how the government would deal with the organization's statewide agenda. In the course of the evening the lieutenant governor underwent what community organizing jargon calls an "accountability session." That means he was presented with a list of the actions the organization had determined to be in the interest of the people. He was then asked to supply a straight up-or-down, monosyllabic, unnuanced and unspun "Yes" or "No" answer to questions such as, "Will you support this measure?" and, given the lieutenant governor's authority over the state senate, "Will you call it up for a vote?"

It was warm in the crowded gymnasium and the lieutenant governor was visibly uncomfortable. He was a bull-like man in a gray suit and as the evening wore on the region above his white collar bulged and his face reddened. The bills he was called to account for included fair funding of public education, utility services for the "shanty towns" on the Mexican border, and state-sponsored health care for the indigent.

Historically, Texas politics have embodied the worst elements of the Southern plantation and the Western frontier. The lower classes were subject to the paternalism of a business class that was accustomed to getting what it wanted by any means necessary. Jan Wilbur, a stout, gray-haired, white woman, and a TMO leader, recalls that when the organization began in Houston, "The president of the Chamber of Commerce and former mayor led a crusade against TMO...saying...'The business community has always looked after the citizens of Houston. There is no reason to get the citizens involved.'

"I began to realize," Wilbur continued, "that they were afraid of the possibility that African American, white, and Hispanic people might join together to work for their common interests—housing, education, fair utility rates, better neighborhoods...that resources might be used for the good of all, instead of for the benefit of just a few."

In small but significant ways that was exactly what started to happen in Texas in the later 1980s. In Houston and the other cities, the IAF organizations registered new voters and brought new citizen leaders into the arena. They transformed politics by creating a new political public, or "civil society."

This new reality was embodied in broad-based "people power" organizations, firmly rooted in the churches, with which politicians and business leaders were forced to contend as equals.

This was an entirely new thing in Texas. The citizens' organizations were effective because they had real institutional power in the churches and especially because they were so broad-based. Unlike traditional liberal or conservative lobbies, the congregation-based organizations did not speak for one region, or one aggrieved ethnic group, or a single-issue special interest. Instead, they spoke for a representative coalition of citizens—urban, suburban and rural; middle class and poor; black, white and brown—who were motivated by common interests and values.

Suddenly, in one of the most conservative states in the union, issues such as health care and utilities for the poorest members of the community entered the political mainstream. And those issues came to the fore with the support of middle-class church people who, five years earlier, may not have known that Texas had shanty towns. White middle-class Texans found themselves drawn into a relationship of mutual cooperation and solidarity with the poor brown people who lived in those shantytowns. This relationship was built on the basis of faith, but also on the basis of a common self-interest in improving the quality of life in the community they shared.

The mayor of Houston was at the TMO meeting, too. She was questioned about proposals to introduce zoning laws in that notoriously laissez-faire city. Black and Mexican-American families wanted no more drinking establishments in their residential areas. Middle-class whites wanted their subdivisions protected from commercial and industrial blight. People from all three communities were concerned about air and water pollution from the city's petroleum industry.

On all these issues, and more, the organized citizens of Houston presented a united front. They were in a pact in which the cause of one became the concern of all. With that power they made change.

## One Church at a Time

There is an old saying that God must really love the common people because He made so many of them. That proverb, or cliché, holds the key to the workings of church-based community organizations. Ordinary citizens may have little money or access to the institutions of power. But they can have power through their numbers and through the practice of their faith. Congregation-based organizations work on the principle that the vast majority of people have more in common than they have dividing them. Furthermore, those common people, the democratic majority, are seen to have shared interests which are not being served by their public institutions.

During the 1992 transition, President Clinton solicited advice from a number of community leaders. One of them was PICO founder Rev. John Baumann, S.J. In a memo to the new president and his staff Baumann wrote, "There is a growing estrangement taking place in our society. Simply stated, this estrangement is between the 'haves and the have-nots.' It is between those who have a stake in our society and those who do not. . . . It is between those who can shape their own futures and those who have none to shape."

When this situation has arisen in the past, popular organizations have been formed to fight for the interests of the average citizen. These organizations were usually rooted in the workplace (unions) or the geographic community of farming regions or urban neighborhoods. But in America today interests are often confused and communities are difficult to define. The established institutions of government and business are not serving the people, but neither are the old modes of popular organization.

The 1960s and 1970s saw the birth of movements based on ethnicity, lifestyle affinities, or the popular issues of the day, but those have not been effective replacements for the organized unions and communities of the past. Such movements often depended on the personality and leadership of a single charismatic individual. The movements withered away when the leader left the scene or was removed from it. Others built around a single hot topic, such as the Vietnam War or nuclear power, faded away when the single-issue battle was won or lost.

By definition most of these movements limited their appeal either to members of a certain ethnic group or gender, or to people with the leisure time to cultivate and pursue special interests. Unlike the workplace or community organizations of the past, the concerns of these movements were seen as distant from the daily lives of the majority of Americans.

From the 1930s to the early 1970s the industrial union movement was the most important institution representing the broad interests of most Americans. The unions are marginalized now. Their membership, as a percentage of the work force, is approximately one-quarter of what it was in the 1950s. A comeback for the unions will not be quick or easy. In the post-industrial economy the workplace is speeded-up and fragmented. The world of work is downsized, outsourced, and temped, as the jargon goes. Even people who have jobs may have a shaky sense of exactly who they work for or with. Workplace organization is more difficult than it has ever been.

At the same time, ordinary people have an intuition that their sense of powerlessness and downward drift is driven by something bigger and more complex than the facts of their particular job or the events of their immediate area. Something new and bewildering is happening in the TV-soaked, two-job lives of the suburban American family. It results from the convergence of declining incomes, media saturation, and the scattering of the time available for and functions formerly held by family life into the marketplace of work and consumption.

In this world, the poor are seen as a threatening subculture accused of murder on the evening news. The rich are those beautiful people on TV who set the standards and the rules. The neighbors are just the people you pass in the car. This makes for a disorienting life, at best, and the people to whom this is happening are without the resources of extended family and community that may have brought their ancestors through earlier trials.

At the very dawn of this new era of decline, in the late 1970s, IAF organizer Ed Chambers analyzed the scene in the following terms. There is, he wrote, "a war being waged...over who will shape the values of our society. It is about this fundamental question: Who will parent our children?...Will this parenting take place in a strictly secular setting where profit is the sole standard of judgment?"

In words that, from a distance of two decades, read as prophecy, Chambers suggested that "the economic and political middle of this country is being sucked dry by a vacuum— a vacuum of power and values. Into that vacuum have moved the huge corporations, mass media and 'benevolent' government...." This has occurred, Chambers says, because "the churches and unions were not prepared for the new institutional arrangements and technologies that have overwhelmed us....Without effective institutional power of their own, families and churches withdraw, backbite [and] blame each other."

In the early days of community organizing, when Alinsky wrote his rulebook, it was assumed that people had to be organized on the basis of their immediate material self-interest. Church-based organizers have now refined this precept with the understanding that, in reality, people's interests are defined by their values. And people's values are both material and moral.

For instance, most people value a certain standard of living for their family and an education for their children. We might call these material values. Most people also value freedom and human dignity and a sense of responsibility. Those are moral values. But in the arena of the family and local community the moral and material—values and interests— intersect. A decent standard of living for one's family means economic development that will contribute to the overall prosperity of the community. For most people, a good education for their children is inextricably linked with the fate of the public schools.

IAF's Texas coordinator Ernesto Cortes calls this the conjunction of "the world as it should be," ruled by love, and "the world as it is," ruled by power. Both love and power are necessary. "Both come from God," he says. "They both are part of creation." But when they are out of alignment, love becomes mere sentiment, power becomes oppression, and legitimate self-interest deteriorates into selfishness. When love and power work together, self-interest leads us into relationship with others, because only in a community of relationships can our deepest values be acted out and our truest self-interest realized.

Over generations of community organizing work, the smartest organizers have learned that churches, synagogues, and religious congregations are the places where most people's values and interests come together. They are the places where families convene to affirm the things that are important to them. Those families bring money to the church to further those values, and this gives congregations a measure of material power and permanence. Religious congregations are also the places where citizen-leaders are often already functioning on boards of deacons or elders or parish councils. And, at the deepest level, places of worship supply the moral grounding that is needed to maintain a balance between the world as it is and the world as it should be.

Now, in hundreds of cities and towns across the country, people are becoming active, through their congregations, in improving the life of their community alongside others who share their fundamental Judeo-Christian values.

At this writing, five different national and regional networks are involved full time in building congregation-based organizations. These organizations involve 1,800 congregations nationwide with an estimated total of 1.5 million Americans of every ethnic background and economic status. The California-based PICO, for instance, puts out figures stating that its membership is 38 percent Hispanic, 33 percent white, 21 percent black, and 7 percent Asian. PICO's member families are classified as 37 percent working class, 29 percent middle class, and 12 percent low income.

Each of the networks building congregation-based organizations has its own twist on the organizing process. But in most cases the pattern is still remarkably similar. An organizing committee of local pastors invites in an organizer. From the beginning, the organizing committee is required to be ethnically and ecumenically representative of the community. Member churches must commit money to fund the first stage of the organizing, which can last for two years.

Next comes an exhaustive series of meetings. One to one, and in small groups, the leaders in each congregation are identified and trained. They in turn meet with others to identify and define the problems facing the community. Problems and possible solutions are researched by the people themselves. From this process an issue and a plan of action will emerge from the bottom up. Piece by painstaking piece, over a period of two years or so, an organization emerges that can speak for the people in the language of their best hopes and dreams. At last the organization is ready to go public and to begin transforming the life of the community.

When the congregation-based organization becomes a public entity, it still does not solicit or accept individual memberships from the general public. Instead, people become involved through the vehicle of their local religious congregation. In some cases civic groups are allowed to affiliate. But the membership, and the power base, is always institutional.

The Texas IAF Network states a goal of "building broad-based organizations of people from diverse faiths and ethnic backgrounds. With broad-based institutionalized power, IAF organizations relate to a community's other power centers, such as government, corporations, banks and school systems."

The focus of church-based organizing is kept on immediate winnable issues. Sometimes the congregation groups begin by taking action on issues they have identified as important for their immediate area. The groups from the congregations also begin meeting and acting in coalition with other congregations from throughout the city. These coalition groups are always city- or area-wide and interracial from the outset. As a result, bridges between black, white, and brown neighborhoods and churches are built from the start. In some cities these bridges also extend from the poor inner city to the middle-class suburbs.

In such racially divided cities as New Orleans, Memphis, and Atlanta, the very existence of a broad-based interracial organization has represented an important beacon of hope. In Washington, DC, the recent emergence of the interracial, IAF-organized Washington Interfaith Network (WIN) was seen by many observers as a surprising and important first step in constructing a non-racial politics for the nation's troubled capital.

In New York, a leader of the Queens Citizens Organization identified himself with a famous Queens-dwelling TV bigot when he admitted frankly, "I'm Archie Bunker." But, he added, in the citizens organization "we've buried the stereotypes by sharing the same values—values of family, neighborhood, congregation—by empowering our people to act upon those values. We broke the language barrier by speaking a common language, a language of diversity, dignity, self-respect, and power."

As IAF's Ed Chambers has written, an alliance of churches can negotiate successfully with banks and insurance companies and media institutions. It "can open up the doors of corporate America and government bureaucracy." In the process of winning tangible victories for the ordinary people, he adds, "the citizens' organization serves as a forum for city-dwellers and suburbanites, blacks and Hispanics and whites, transforming words like 'ecumenicity' and 'racial equality' into flesh and blood realities."

The process of church-based community organizing has become replicated so many times now that it is almost formulaic. But it is a formula that works. It produces community spirit and steps toward social justice. It rekindles the best of the American democratic tradition. It brings people together, and lets them be their best and truest selves. It demonstrates, in concrete, face-to-face action, that the things ordinary black, white, and brown people have in common are more important and powerful than the things that drive them apart.

We all know that power corrupts. It is the oldest political cliché in the book. But, as Ernesto Cortes has pointed out, "power-lessness corrupts, too." Powerlessness is the plague of our turn-of-the-century America. It is the father to our culture of cynicism and violence. Powerlessness is the common denominator of the angry white males of militia-land and the angry black males of inner-city gangs. Powerlessness is the void that the middle class may try to fill with another credit card or another cable channel. The welfare mother may try to fill that same void with another child.

Powerlessness is the plague that makes us hate each other when we can't control, or even understand, what is happening to ourselves. In America today people who work hard and play by the rules don't get ahead anymore. The jobs those people used to do are gone. The majority is sinking into debt and permanent decline. The poor minority is sinking into desperation. The world we thought we knew has been taken away from us. We don't even know where it went and we can't seem to do a thing about it. We try a new president or a new Congress, as if they were a new drug. But the medicine doesn't work.

None of our diversions are effective substitutes for power. Power is the ability to speak with our own voice and walk with our own feet and mark our own image of God across the face of the earth. We can't live without it. It, alongside love, is what makes us human.

The church-based organizations may not have all of the answers to everything that plagues America. But when they talk about powerlessness they have made the right diagnosis. And when they talk about more democracy they are onto a prescription.

CHAPTER 9

# No Time Like the Present

## The Hammer and the Wedge

In the wake of the conservative tide in the November 1994 congressional elections, the media and political professionals discovered something they called "the angry white male." This is a person previously encountered in these pages under the generic title of the "American worker," or as the father and husband of the "average family." In the conventional wisdom of the moment, this person is supposed to be enraged, not by a loss of jobs and income, but by the perceived preferences that big government extends to minorities and women.

Newt Gingrich and company are playing the affirmative action issue like bullfighters. With one hand they brandish the issue as a red flag in the white man's face. Meanwhile, with the other hand, they hand out tax breaks and deregulation freebies to global corporations. These are the very same corporations that are in the business of downsizing the American economy and decreasing real economic opportunity for Americans of all colors.

As this is written, a movement is afoot to put an anti-affirmative action initiative on the 1996 ballot in California. In Louisiana a new Republican governor has abolished affirmative action in state government. Various proposals to eliminate federal affirmative action requirements are rattling around the Republican Congress. All signs point to a propaganda crescendo around the issue, timed to peak during the 1996 campaigns.

With their strict abolitionist proposals on affirmative action, the conservatives hope to do with that issue what both sides did with abortion, i.e., to polarize the issue and force people into unnuanced positions defending or rejecting the status quo. In fact the polls indicate that, as with abortion, most people, including lots of black people, have mixed feelings about affirmative action. Most of white America seems to recognize that some safeguards are still necessary to make sure that African Americans have access to the mainstream. But most of them are also uncomfortable with the idea of permanently codifying preferences based on color.

The Right hopes to blow past the nuances and maximize the discomfort level. Conservative Republicans are counting on affirmative action to serve as the wedge issue that will reopen the White House doors and postpone a serious discussion of America's economic condition for at least another four years. They believe that affirmative action is *the* hot issue of the decade and they are going to hammer it hard.

It is a hot issue, and not just because there is still racism in America. It is also a troublesome question because the idea of making decisions based on race *sounds* wrong. Even the most fervent supporters of affirmative action must realize that it is a concept intensely vulnerable to caricature and scapegoating. The very invention of the euphemistic name is a concession to this fact.

After twenty-five years, affirmative action has become a ubiquitous part of American life. Anyone who has applied to schools or looked for a job lately has confronted those forms asking for the applicant's race and gender. As the years have worn on, the affirmative action status categories have proliferated to include the handicapped, the Vietnam-era veteran, the over-40 and a variety of "new immigrant" ethnic groups. The small print on those affirmative action forms always says that the information is confidential and purely for statistical purposes. But in this age of bureaucracy run amok it is hard to blame people for drawing more sinister conclusions.

In the end, the social progress from affirmative action is relatively small. In the early days it helped create the black middle class and helped open doors for women. But the path up the economic ladder is largely blocked for everyone now. In the future the benefits of affirmative action will be increasingly likely to go to the middle-class sons and daughters of the first affirmative action generation. And in return the programs make people feel that they are being tracked, classified, and judged on the basis of an accident of birth. Even to some good people, this feels like an unfair and unnecessary intrusion.

As long as the national discussion about race revolves around whether one is for or against affirmative action, there will be no progress for anyone. Proposals for class-based affirmative action, replacing ethnic status with family income and education level, make more sense at this juncture in history, and could offer a way past the conundrum. But even then, if we are stuck talking about who will get access to a shrinking number of good jobs, then we are stuck talking about the wrong questions.

Affirmative action has become a "lose-lose" issue. The only people who win in this fight are the well-to-do and powerful. Those are the people who, after four centuries of history, still have a powerful interest in dividing working Americans against each other on the basis of color.

A protracted war over affirmative action in the late 1990s may delay the inevitable, but the facts of American economic decline must eventually be faced. If those facts are to be faced with a just and democratic outcome they must be faced by ordinary black, white, and brown people together, on the basis of their shared self-interest in making a change.

**The Great Disinheritance**

America is in the throes of two long-term crises that are in fact inextricably linked. One is economic. American workers are coming out as losers in the very global economy that their tax dollars and military service helped to create. Under the ideological banner of "free trade" the American manufacturing economy is being shipped overseas, to be replaced with a service economy that provides extravagantly high incomes for the upper tier of elite "knowledge workers" and steadily shrinking prospects for the majority. After almost two decades of denial, the existence of this economic crisis is now at least widely acknowledged.

America's other crisis is cultural. This is the crisis of values that is the bizarre offspring of 1960s counterculturalism and 1980s Republicanism: divorce, family breakdown, commercialization of sex, tolerance of public violence and misogyny, loss of moral moorings and spiritual meaning.

In fact these two crises, the economic and cultural, are inextricably linked. We have a cultural crisis in part because, for most white Americans, our cultural values have always been predicated upon unending economic growth. Since the time of the Puritans, and certainly since the days of Ben Franklin, the rewards of virtue in America were expected to be material. Right behavior was rewarded by prosperity. It was no shame, in this culture, to be born poor. In fact, humble origins were a badge of honor. But to remain poor was to be labeled lazy and foolish. It represented a moral failure. Families were linked across the generations by the steady ascent from the immigrant boat to the professional office or corporate suite.

At the same time the individualist free market ideology that propelled American economic growth held within it the seeds of moral destruction. At first market ideology and morality worked together. On the farm families stuck together because they needed each other for economic productivity. With the Industrial Revolution the modern nuclear family was born. Industry needed the wife to serve as home front support staff for the full-time male worker bee. The children were removed from home, into the schools, to absorb the ideological and practical training required for future home or factory workers.

But after World War II productivity was no longer the problem. Our productive capacity far outstripped the markets for our goods. To redress this balance, the market system had to encourage consumption, and the moral equation was reversed. In a consumption economy it is better for families to break up. Smaller, more fragmented households mean more purchases of home appliances, electronic goods, automobiles, and all the other big ticket items that make our economy go 'round.

This economic trend met its cultural match in the 1960s counterculture. "Do your own thing" translated very neatly into "buy your own things." "If it feels good, do it" was a consumer slogan made for the credit card age. The enduring commercial legacy of the counterculture is plain in everything from rock and roll car commercials to Coca Cola's psychedelic graphics and Pepsi's eternal generational gap.

In the lives of ordinary Americans the counterculture legacy is most visible in America's changed sexual morality. In essence, the 1960s can be remembered as the time when Americans on a mass scale began to apply the values of the marketplace (instant gratification and convenience) to the arena of sexual behavior and family life. It became acceptable to shed inconvenient partners and children. Our divorce laws changed to accommodate consumer demand.

An entire generation grew up expecting literally to shop around for personal fulfillment. These changes began among the children of the elite in the 1960s. Over the next two decades they filtered out to the middle class and the poor with disastrous consequences for everyone.

Then, starting in the mid-1970s, the generation of the 1960s, and the one to follow, encountered the double whammy of economic stagnation. The stable two-parent families that managed to survive were punished for their trouble. By the early 1980s most of them were forced to send both parents into the workplace in order to maintain a shaky grip on middle-class status. Parents looked on with impotent befuddlement as the rearing of their children was turned over to the daycare industry, school bureaucracies, and the electronic culture of videos, computer games, and cable TV.

And still the tide of prosperity continued to ebb. As the calendar rolled on into the 1990s Americans looked around and discovered that the bottom had dropped out of the life they expected. This experience did not rival the Great Depression in its suddenness and severity. But we could call it the Great Disinheritance. The legacy that America promised its free white inhabitants for more than 200 years, and that it recently extended to African Americans, has been abruptly withdrawn.

It is as if we all had a wealthy old relative we depended upon to tend the family business and distribute the family wealth. Let's call him Uncle Sam. Then Uncle Sam died and at the reading of the will we discovered that the estate was passing into other hands. To sharpen the analogy, let's say that the inheritance was handed over to some international commission of professional bureaucrats and financiers.

When something like this happens, Americans, true to the gospel of prosperity, will automatically assume that they have done something to bring this bad fortune upon themselves. Many will despair and descend into self-destruction. When a period of breast-beating has passed, some of the children and cousins might begin to squabble viciously among themselves, each convinced that the other must be responsible for the disinheritance.

This rancor might last a long time, maybe even for an entire generation. But one day Uncle Sam's descendants will have to stop bickering and come together to rebuild their family ties. They may be disinherited, but without those ties that bind they are dehumanized, which is even worse. When family ties are renewed, attention can turn to the creation of a new family business. And in this new family arrangement everyone will have a hand in the work and the decisions. Nobody will trust everything to a friendly rich uncle again.

### Running the Numbers

The first step to putting the pieces of American life back together is to recognize who and what we really are. A few years back there was a country song that said, sagely, "the stars may lie, but the numbers never do." The song was about horoscopes and lottery tickets, but the proverb applies here, because the true portrait of the class-based multiracial constituency for a new America is written in the numbers, not the stars.

Between 1979 and 1993, according to the U.S. Census, the bottom three-fifths, or 60 percent, of American households suffered a real loss of income. In the national aggregate, real household income grew between 1979 and 1993 by $767 billion, but 97 percent of the increase went to the richest one-fifth of American households.

Those numbers are at the very core of the discontent and anger loose in America today. They inscribe in black and white the living truth that, for all but a few, the American dream has been canceled. Those numbers represent a powerful community of interest waiting to discover itself. The bottom three-fifths of the population includes all of the manufacturing workers in America, all of the skilled craftspersons, all of the technicians and mechanics, all of the clerical workers in government, business, and nonprofit agencies, and most of the teachers and public service employees.

The lower 60 percent includes everyone except the professional class and the super-rich whom they serve. The professional class includes the traditional corps of doctors, lawyers, and bankers, plus the knowledge and information elite of the media and high-tech industries. This crew is so outnumbered that in any real democracy they would be a pitiful fringe group cowering for cover behind their BMWs. But, for now, they set economic policy and cultural standards, at least until an organized majority finds its public voice and a democratic vocabulary that fits the times.

Thirty years ago it was not inappropriate to base a campaign for democratic social change on the notion that white middle-class Americans needed to make room at the table for blacks and the poor. But that vocabulary no longer matches reality. Today the middle class and the poor, regardless of ethnicity, are simply riding in different parts of the same boat. And the ship is going down. They are all part of that great three-fifths majority.

If there is not a substantial rearrangement of economic life, the middle class will continue to lose income and see its family life and communal values consumed by the struggle to stay ahead of the bills. The poor will have no hope of escaping their circumstances and will sink deeper into family breakdown, crime, and the other diseases of despair.

For the first fifteen years of American economic decline the white middle class blamed itself for its troubles. They tried to fix their declining income by their own determined efforts. They resolved to work harder. They took second jobs. They sent additional family members out into the workforce. That is the way Americans have always gotten through hard times.

But in this case the good times didn't come back, and finally, with the great middle-class recession of 1991, ordinary white Americans started looking for someone to blame. They blamed George Bush, and his administration deserved it. Now they blame Bill Clinton, and it hardly seems to matter any more whether his administration deserves it or not. Soon they will blame Newt Gingrich. Persistently some of them blame the immigrants, the people on welfare, the feminists, the criminals —"them." And we all know who "they" are.

But that blaming of fellow victims has not yet caught on as virulently as it has at some times in the past. In part that is because the absurdity of it is more apparent than in most times past. Clearly the people in the inner city, the immigrants, and all of the non-white "others" are not doing so well these days themselves. It is hard to muster even anecdotal evidence to the contrary.

In addition, the appetite and market for bigotry in America is simply not as strong as it was at earlier times in our history such as the 1930s. There is more of a common working assumption in America that people should not be judged by ethnicity and color. Discrimination still happens, of course, but even the people who discriminate claim to believe that it is wrong. This makes it harder for a race-baiting analysis of American decline to take hold.

This is mostly a legacy of the moral battle that was won in the 1960s. Things will have to get a lot worse before racism can masquerade as The American Way in a country that has placed Martin Luther King, Jr. alongside Lincoln and Washington in its civil pantheon. The changed atmosphere also reflects the influence of the racially mixed popular culture that has grown up in America in the past forty years and has become our new Statue of Liberty to the world.

Given these two intimately related historical developments, there is more of a cultural basis for interracial cooperation in America today than there has been at any time since William met Mary in seventeenth-century Virginia. When this cultural foundation is placed alongside the convergence of economic self-interest represented by declining incomes, the potential for a new American revolution becomes obvious. This American revolution, like all the ones that have come before it, will be about the preservation and extension of democracy. It will be about taming the institutions of economic and cultural power so that they serve the moral and material interests of the majority.

Both the poor and the middle class have an interest in changing the American economy. The core change of direction that is required is a turn toward a policy of reindustrialization. We need to rebuild and update America's basic manufacturing capacity. This could be done through a combination of worker education and training and targeted tax subsidies and trade protections for domestic manufacturing.

Rebuilding America's manufacturing base will also require that we roll back the tide of corporate globalism and begin to hold American corporations accountable to the needs of American families and communities. This may mean rewriting some of the international trade agreements, such as the North American Free Trade Agreement (NAFTA) and the General Agreement on Tariffs and Trade (GATT) that were designed to facilitate the mobility of jobs and capital.

A rebirth of American manufacturing would lift the boats of virtually everyone in the bottom three-fifths of America. It would put some of the old underemployed industrial work force back on the job at something like their former wages. Retrained managers would be in demand, too, although the lines between workers, technicians, and managers will inevitably blur in the high-tech industrial future.

A new American manufacturing economy would open a door out of poverty for the young of the inner city. The children of moderate-income towns and suburbs and the children of the inner city would have a new name for each other. They might still use some of the old ethnic handles. But they would also have to call each other co-worker. That change would make a difference in the American atmosphere. And maybe, if a new industrial unionism emerged in America, those co-workers of many colors might find themselves calling each other "brother" and "sister" again.

A reindustrialization policy alone would be enough to set the ball rolling. Once lower- and moderate-income people are re-enfranchised as actors in the system, many of the other changes our economy and society need—like health care reform, a family policy to subsidize traditional two-parent homes, a serious across-the-board commitment to public schools— would begin to fall into place. An empowered constituency for those changes would make progress possible.

A new level of security, stability, and self-respect for the working middle class would also make it possible to extend new, more thoughtful and respectful efforts toward restoring the minority of our people who bear crippling damage from lives of poverty and discrimination and from the dependency induced by the current welfare system.

**Redrawing the Lines**

The words came from the mouth of a young, evangelical Christian, white woman from the Midwest. The young woman had taken a year off from college to work in the presidential campaign of Pat Buchanan. She understood that Buchanan had little chance to win, she said, but she insisted, "If you are pro-family and pro-life, anti-NAFTA and anti-GATT, he is the only choice."

I read it and nearly wept. That idealistic young woman had cut straight to the core of the new era in American political culture. Her politics are defined by the twin specters of American cultural and economic decline. On one side of the pit she sees the sexual individualism of abortion, divorce, and illegitimacy, and the reduction of human values to "the right to control one's own body." On the other side looms the economic individualism of free trade and capital flight.

That young woman sees no one standing up for the values of human dignity and communal responsibility. She hears no voices speaking for the right to life and the right to work. No one, that is, except Pat Buchanan, and that is why I wanted to cry. Pat Buchanan is one of the most widely heard voices in current American politics speaking out against the global corporations and the free trade ideology. He has cast himself as the working man's conservative. But many working women are offended by his antediluvian social views, and black and brown workers know that his vision does not include them.

The emergence of a Buchanan in the American political mainstream points to the dangers that can arise when people's real interests are not being addressed in a multiracial democratic context. But it also points to the fact that "free trade" and corporate globalism could become issues even hotter than affirmative action. Those could, in fact, become wedge issues separating cultural conservatives from their contradictory alliance with free market ideologues.

When the history of our strange turn-of-the-century era is written, the debates over the North American Free Trade Agreement (NAFTA) and the General Agreement on Tariffs and Trade (GATT) may well be seen as the signal events of the day. NAFTA established unrestricted trade between the United States, Canada, and Mexico. In so doing it removed Mexican restrictions on U.S. goods and services and made it easier for American factories to move to Mexico and take advantage of lower wages and looser regulations. GATT rewrote the terms of trade in the post-Cold War world in a way that lowered most of the old barriers between markets (or "nations," as they were once called). It also established a World Trade Organization (WTO) and made the economic policies of the member nations subject to the review and approval of this unelected and unaccountable body.

The 1993 debate on ratification of the North American Free Trade Agreement was the hardest fought of these two globalist battles in the United States. And the NAFTA struggle suggested some of the outlines of a new political culture of common economic interests. Opposition to NAFTA brought together African American leaders, trade unionists, consumer groups, farmers, environmentalists, and Third World human rights advocates.

Ross Perot, Pat Buchanan, Ralph Nader and Jesse Jackson were all on the same side in the NAFTA struggle. Many media-anointed experts professed to be baffled at such strange bedfellows. But it should have been predictable. NAFTA sharply focused the direct opposition of interests between the globalist corporations and the average American. As a result, a large number of average Americans responded, crossing all the predictable lines of race and ideology that, according to the experts, are supposed to define, and contain, their citizenship.

In the end, NAFTA and GATT were passed by the U.S. Congress not because the people wanted them but because they were shoved through the Congress by an overpowering combination of international corporate money and muscle. But as the loss of American jobs and incomes continues, the question, "Who benefits from the global economy?" will come more to the forefront of American politics.

So far the debate over free trade suggests that it is possible for all of the various, many-shaped and multicolored American households with incomes under $50,000 to recognize their common stake in the long-term economic crisis. At the same time, as the presence of a Pat Buchanan in the anti-NAFTA crowd suggests, the NAFTA debate also pointed to the dangers of an ethnocentric American protectionism. "America First" (Buchanan's slogan) can and will be raised as a weapon, not just against globalist economic plans, but also against non-white immigrants and other "un-Americans."

The way to fight that new xenophobia, however, is not to claim that the Americans who fall prey to it are simply selfish and bigoted. Some of them may be that, but that is not *all* that they are. They are also people with legitimate fears and real grievances that have gone ignored and unaddressed. The debate about corporate globalism is an opportunity for white Americans to see the interest that they share, not only with black and brown workers in the U.S., but also with workers in Latin America and elsewhere who are concerned for the sovereignty and self-sufficiency of their own countries.

Opposition to free trade is not an anti-Third World position. The place of the poor nations of the southern hemisphere in the globalist scheme of things is to supply cheap labor and a passively receptive market for Western goods and culture. In southern Mexico many poor people in the Zapatista army decided to fight NAFTA with real guns, and many more supported that action.

To media gurus the politics of NAFTA in the United States was incomprehensible because they didn't follow the usual liberal-conservative or racial lines. Bill Clinton was for it and Pat Buchanan was against it. Jesse Jackson was against it and former Urban League president Vernon Jordan was for it. Billionaire union buster Ross Perot lined up against NAFTA alongside the leadership of the American labor movement. This confusion was emblematic of the new era of American politics in which all of the old bets are off and anything is possible.

### What's Race Got To Do with It?

What does all this have to do with race? Everything. There will be an ongoing and increasingly self-conscious American middle-class backlash against The Great Disinheritance. This could be good news or bad. Like the girl with the curl, if it is good it will be very, very good. It will take the form of an interracial coalition to reorder America's priorities for the benefit of families and communities. This could become a high point in the story of the American experiment.

If the reaction is bad, it will be very, very bad. To obscure the true sources of American decline, demagogues will exacerbate cultural and racial divisions to the point of civil war. Whole generations of Americans will surrender to the self-destructive diseases of despair. Life will cheapen. Public life and public goods (e.g., parks, highways, waterways, schools) will deteriorate as the public sector shrivels from neglect.

Everything about these two possible outcomes depends upon how the racial politics of our time play out. The question ultimately will be: Can we rise to common ground? Or will we remain mired in backbiting and blaming? Will we find an interracial basis for reconceiving America? Or will we break down into warring fiefdoms? Will the powerless many unite against the wealthy and powerful few? Or will they continue to turn their anger on each other and on those even weaker than themselves?

The possibilities for either direction are present among us. Both directions have precedents in the American story. The argument of this book is that the circumstances have never been better for unity, community, and democracy to prevail.

America's visible and clearly understood economic decline means that it is possible, for the first time since the 1930s, that a significant number of white people may see their economic interests as being in line with, and being furthered by, the aspirations of black and brown people. The changes of the Second Reconstruction, that is, the lowering of racial barriers and the entry of black and white Americans into a more common culture, make it possible for that to happen on a basis that is more equal than ever before in our history.

It is now possible to think in terms of an American majority that is defined in economic and cultural terms, and not racial ones. "Majority" doesn't have to mean "white" anymore. It can, and should, mean the vast multiracial majority of American households—white, black and brown—who have declining incomes and an interest in changing the balance of economic and political power. History demonstrates that it is at least possible for such a majority to act on behalf of its own interests. In the process it can also upset all of the moralistic liberal stereotypes about race and class in America.

The time is ripe for such an overarching unity of interests. The moral ground was prepared by the civil rights movement's progress against overt racism and by the language of civic idealism that it introduced. The task before us is to build on that foundation to help Americans in the 1990s, and beyond, face each other, so that they may face together the common enemy of economic inequality and decline.

For white people of social conscience and egalitarian impulses, the task today is not to browbeat our fellow Americans with their supposed moral inadequacies about race. The task we face is much harder. We have to listen to our fellow Americans and try to hear what they are really saying. We need to drop the old model of rich white relinquishment and poor black empowerment. It comes from another time and that time is over.

Forced downward mobility is now a fact of life for most white Americans. Preaching voluntary downward mobility to them is the height of absurdity. Talking about an "option for the poor" in the United States, as many religious leftists still do, makes even less sense. For one thing, that slogan was coined for Latin American societies in which the poor might be 85 percent of the population. It makes sense in that context. In the U.S. the proportions are reversed and an option for the poor is an option for fringe status. In Latin America people may have a certain healthy pride in identifying themselves as "the poor." It is equivalent to identifying oneself with "the people" as opposed to the elite. But in the U.S. even most people who *are* poor don't call themselves "the poor." In the U.S. the poor want to be middle class like everybody else.

The "option for the poor" rhetoric in the U.S. socio-economic context only creates false divisions that are irrelevant to the real lives and real problems of ordinary Americans. In its place we need to project to our people the possibility of a common struggle for common interests. We need, in essence, to return to the old labor union motto that "an injury to one is an injury to all." We need to reclaim and revive the principle of the common good as handed down in Catholic social teaching. That motto and principle can be applied in practical terms to the issues that are really bothering people in America. It is the only way that we can go forward together.

The stories retold in this book from the American past demonstrate that a new thing has always been present on our American shores, waiting to be born. It is possible for that new thing to happen in our time. The weather is right for it to grow.

In the 1930s the great African American poet, Langston Hughes, reflected on the promise and failure of the American democratic dream. He wrote, "America never was America to me." But in the same breath he vowed, "America will be." It is possible for us here at the end of what was to have been the American century to begin to think again, with the poet, of the America that never was, but must be.

# Sources

## Chapter 2: Revolt before Race

Warren M. Billings, ed., *The Old Dominion in the Seventeenth Century: A Documentary History of Virginia, 1606-1689* (Chapel Hill, N.C.: University of North Carolina Press, 1975).
———, "The Cases of Fernando and Elizabeth Key: A Note on the Status of Blacks in 17th Century Virginia," *William and Mary Quarterly*, 3rd ser., 30 (1973):467-74.
Wesley Frank Craven, *The Southern Colonies in the Seventeenth Century, 1607-1689* (Baton Rouge: Louisiana State University Press, 1949).
William Waller Hening, ed., *The Laws of Virginia* (New York: R. & W. & G. Partow, 1823).
Edmund S. Morgan, *American Slavery, American Freedom: The Ordeal of Colonial Virginia* (New York: W.W. Norton, 1975).
*Virginia Magazine of History and Biography*, SV (1907-1908), 38-43.
Thomas Jefferson Wertenbaker, *Patrician and Plebian in Virginia* (New York: Russell & Russell, 1958).
———, *Virginia under the Stuarts* (Princeton: Princeton University Press, 1914).
Howard Zinn, *A People's History of the United States* (New York: Harpercollins, 1980).

## Chapter 3: A Sign of Contradiction

J. Winston Coleman, *Slavery Times in Kentucky* (Chapel Hill, N.C.: University of North Carolina Press, 1940).

Lowell H. Harrison, *The Antislavery Movement in Kentucky* (Lexington: University Press of Kentucky, 1978).

Elisabeth S. Peck, *Berea's First 125 Years: 1855-1980* (Lexington: University Press of Kentucky, 1982).

Will Frank Steely, "William Shreve Bailey, Kentucky Abolitionist," *Filson Club Historical Quarterly*, 31 July 1957, pp. 274-81.


## Chapter 4: "Separately Fleeced"

Robert L. Allen, *Reluctant Reformers* (New York: Anchor Books, 1975).

Richard Boyer and Herbert Morais, *Labor's Untold Story* (New York: United Electrical, Radio, and Machine Workers of America, 1955).

Charles Crowe, "Tom Watson, Populists and Blacks Reconsidered," *Journal of Negro History*, April 1970.

Barbara Fields, "Ideology and Race in American History," in J. Morgan Kousser, ed., *Region, Race and Reconstruction: Essays in Honor of C. Vann Woodward* (New York: Oxford University Press, 1982).

C. Vann Woodward, *Origins of the New South* (Baton Rouge: Louisiana State University Press, 1951).

————, *Tom Watson: Agrarian Rebel* (New York: Rinehart and Company, 1938).


## Chapter 5: "We Shall Not Be Moved"

Danny Duncan Collum, ed., *African Americans in the Spanish Civil War* (New York: G.K. Hall, 1992).

Anthony Dunbar, *Against the Grain: Southern Radicals and Prophets 1929-1959* (Charlottesville: University Press of Virginia, 1980).

Henry Hampton, producer, *The Great Depression* (Boston: Blackside Productions, Television Series).

H. L. Mitchell, *Mean Things Happening in This Land* (Montclair, N.J.: Methuen, 1979).

## Chapter 6: Making Room at the Table

Barbara Ehrenreich, *Fear of Falling* (New York: Pantheon, 1989).

David J. Garrow, *Bearing the Cross* (New York: Random House, 1986).

Vincent Harding, *Martin Luther King: The Inconvenient Hero* (Maryknoll, N.Y.: Orbis Books, 1996).

Stephen B. Oates, *Let the Trumpet Sound* (New York: Harper & Row, 1982).

# Index

164681

DE PAUL UNIVERSITY LIBRARY

3 0511 00594 2743